MISTAKE in Identity

MISTAKE in Identity

A Cultural Studies
Murder Mystery

Arthur Asa Berger

ALTAMIRA
PRESS

A Division of
ROWMAN & LITTLEFIELD PUBLISHERS, INC.
Lanham • New York • Toronto • Oxford

AltaMira Press
A Division of Rowman & Littlefield Publishers, Inc.
A wholly owned subsidiary of The Rowman & Littlefield Group, Inc.
4501 Forbes Boulevard, Suite 200
Lanham, MD 20706
www.altamirapress.com

PO Box 317, Oxford, OX2 9RU, UK

British Library Cataloguing in Publication Information Available

Library of Congress Cataloging-in-Publication Data

Berger, Arthur Asa, 1933–
    Mistake in identity : a cultural studies murder mystery / Arthur A. Berger.
        p. cm.
    Includes bibliographical references.
    ISBN 0-7591-0864-1 (cloth : alk. paper) — ISBN 0-7591-0865-X (pbk. : alk.
paper)
    1. Culture—Study and teaching—Fiction. I. Title.
    PS3602.E753M57 2005
    813'.54—dc22

                                                                    2005008932

Printed in the United States of America

∞™ The paper used in this publication meets the minimum requirements of
American National Standard for Information Sciences—Permanence of Paper for
Printed Library Materials, ANSI/NISO Z39.48-1992.

For my wife, Phyllis Wolfson Berger

table of **contents**

preface and **acknowledgments**

A number of years ago, Mitch Allen, president of AltaMira Press (otherwise known as "The Great Rejecter"), suggested that, since I am an artist as well as a writer, I draw and write a comic book on postmodernism. I didn't have any luck with the comic-strip format and decided instead to write an academic mystery on postmodernism and illustrate each chapter with a comic-strip frame. That led to *Postmortem for a Postmodernist*, a darkly humorous mystery about Professor Ettore Gnocchi, who was murdered four different ways on the first page of the book.

It was, I thought, a brave thing for Mitch Allen to publish the book—a mystery novel about postmodernism. Fortunately, it was well received, and that led to my writing other mysteries, such as *The Mass Comm Murders*, in which five media theorists murder one another, and *Durkheim Is Dead: Sherlock Holmes Is Introduced to Sociological Theory*, which is about classical sociological theory.

Now that I've published half a dozen mysteries, I have reidentified myself as a postmodern novelist. That is one of the pleasures of living in a postmodern society—our identities are now fluid, easily changed, always up for grabs, so to speak. (And so, you'll find, are our genders and sexuality.) There was always a question in my mind as to whether I was a teacher who wrote or a writer who taught. In recent years, since 1970, when my first book was published (my Ph.D. dissertation on the comic strip *Li'l Abner*), I've considered myself to be a writer who, by chance, also happened to be a professor.

But it is only since I started writing my mysteries that I've redefined myself as a novelist. Some critics, I should point out, have suggested that all my books—on media, popular culture, humor, research methods, and related subjects—should be considered works of fiction. Like all writers I have discovered that critics are not always kind. One critic, reviewing a book I wrote in the seventies, *The TV-Guided American*, concluded his review with the line "Berger is to the serious study of television what Idi Amin is to tourism in Uganda." It was a nasty assessment but a wonderful line, and it always gets good laughs for me when I quote it in lectures.

This book is a work of fiction. All the characters and situations in the book were invented by me and are the products of my imagination, except, that is, for the cruise ship on which the action takes place—the *Royal Duchess*. (I took a cruise to Alaska on a ship whose name is very similar to that of my imaginary cruise ship, the *Royal Duchess*, in 2000 and had a wonderful time, eating my way from San Francisco to Alaska and back and not gaining any weight to speak of.)

Any resemblance between characters in this book and actual persons, dead or alive, is strictly coincidental. Although *Mistake in Identity* is a work of fiction, you will find that like many other works of fiction, it can tell us a great deal about reality. It focuses on the matter of identity and shows how cultural studies scholars, from a variety of different disciplines, deal with this very problematical subject. Is it gender that is basic? Race? Socioeconomic class? Our postmodern society? Our unconscious? Something else?

I hope that my readers will also find this novel useful in helping them deal with an extremely interesting and important problem, one that we all face—namely, how do we become who we are, how do we form a "self"? I am talking about the mystery of identity. At one time or another we all speculate about our identities. We all wonder who we are and how it was that we turned out the way we did (just lucky, we assume). And we also wonder what changes to our identities we might be making in the future.

So it is identity, and the way cultural studies scholars deal with identity, that is the subject of this murder mystery. It is, like all mysteries, a mystery involving the identity of a murderer, but it is also a mystery about identity, in general. It is, then, in the best postmodern sense (I'll have something to say about postmodernism shortly), a mystery about a mystery.

I hope you enjoy it . . . and learn something from it.

ACKNOWLEDGMENTS

I'd like to thank my editor at AltaMira Press, John O'Brien, and his colleague there, Grace Ebron, for their many helpful and valuable suggestions. I've had a long and very pleasant relationship with Mitch Allen and his colleagues at AltaMira Press and am grateful for their confidence in me and my books. I'd also like to express my appreciation to those members of the staff of AltaMira Press who were involved in publishing this book: my copy editor, Jen Sorenson; my production editor, Janice Braunstein; and my cover designer, Allison Nealon. In addition, I want to thank Douglas Kellner, who reviewed this book in manuscript form, for his many helpful suggestions. Finally, I want to thank Dennis Stempler, MD, for providing me with an autopsy report that I used, in abbreviated and modified form, in this book.

pers**onae**

Marshall McInnis: Amos Birdwhistell Chair of Media Studies at the University of Southern California and a leading scholar in the area of media studies and identity research. He also had a passionate interest in having sex with nubile young women and didn't care whether they were married or single and, if married, to friends of his or not. He organized an experiment. He took a group of scholars he had met on his numerous visiting professorships on a "working cruise" to write a book on "the problem of identity." The experiment ended early for him and not quite the way he thought it would.

Symphonie Wu: professor of sociology at the Beijing Broadcasting Institute and visiting professor at the film department of the University of Southern California. Years earlier she had married McInnis after a short courtship and then divorced him just a few months after they got married, saying she'd made a terrible mistake. She was interested in race and its relationship to identity. Her book on identity and race, *Yellow Skin, White Soul*, was considered an important contribution to the field.

Anastasia Lotman: a Russian scholar, was professor of semiotics at the University of Bologna, where she taught courses on semiotics and

cultural studies. She was divorced from her husband, the late Count Et-
tore Chiodo, and remarried a person from Tartu, where she had studied.
She was about to spend a year as a visiting professor at the University of
California in Los Angeles. She was the author of *Markers: The Semiotics of
Identity*. Her focus was on signs and their relationship to identity.

Jean-Marie Benetton: a member of the prestigious CNRS in France
and a distinguished anthropologist. He had spent years living with various native peoples and writing books about his experiences. He was a
visiting professor at Harvard University in the Department of Social Relations, where he taught a seminar in the culture of postmodernism and
identity. His book *Constructing the Postmodern Self: Gender, Sex, Body, and
the Creation of Identities* was a revolutionary study of the way people create and re-create themselves.

Katarina Mittags: known as the "Red" professor, was head of media
studies at Berlin Technical University. She was famous for a book, *MedienMarx*, that used Marxist theory to analyze German mass media and
popular culture. Her interest was in socioeconomic class and consciousness, with a focus on the sociocultural determinants of identity.

Antonia Fathom: senior reader in literary studies at Oxford University, used rhetorical theory to analyze the portrayal of women in works of
literature and texts in the mass media. She had written an important
book on identity, *The Rhetoric of Identity*, and was at work on a book on
medieval attitudes toward gender. She came from an upper-class English
family and was a leader in the feminist movement in Britain.

Sigfried Duerfklein: professor of psychiatry at the University of Vienna and a leading theorist in the field of identity studies. He was the
editor of *Identity Studies* and author of two of the leading studies in the
field, *The Secret Self: The Psychology of the Impostor* and *Studies in the
Creation of an Identity: An Introduction* (three volumes).

Solomon Hunter: an enigmatic police inspector in San Francisco who dressed in Brooks Brothers suits and loved opera. He had investigated several other murders involving academics and had developed a considerable amount of expertise in dealing with professorial types. Hunter graduated from the University of California at Berkeley and then joined the police force—a surprise to all who knew him.

Talcott Weems: Hunter's assistant, was an anti-intellectual and extremely cynical about people and their motivations. Weems, who had attended San Francisco State University, was a sergeant in the police force. He had an aversion to professors, who are generally, as he put it, "too full of themselves."

"The chorus sings a *complete* account of her career while she has her ear to the keyhole. But I see it's all far above your head. You don't grasp it at all. Not that I do, myself. I would much rather not write the play at all."

"Then why not drop it?"

"How can I, dear? Don't be *too* obtuse. I must know who I am, mustn't I?"

"Surely your own play isn't going to tell you?"

"Of course not, dear; it's the critics who'll tell me. At the moment I don't exist; I don't even know what to *become*. But once my play's done, I'll know. One critic will say: 'Harold Snatogen reveals himself as an embodiment of the fashionable anti-Moon Goddess revival.' Another will say: 'In Snatogen we see what Hegel called . . .'" And then he'll tell what Hegel called. After that it will be quite simple: I shall become the most flattering definition." (217–18)

Nigel Dennis,
Cards of Identity

Marjorie Ferguson and Peter Golding, "Cultural Studies and Changing Times: An Introduction"

If, indeed, cultural studies is in transition, its current stage of evolution is much preoccupied with questions of collective identity. Now identity is a notoriously slippery and multi-dimensional concept, that ranges in this case from the identity of cultural studies itself to those of its theorists and constituencies: the dialogue of difference or sameness within the discourses of feminism, ethnicity, sexual orientation, Eurocentrism, the disaporic, the post-colonial and the post-national. The embrace of identity, and its excavation from the bedrock of personal history, adds perhaps another mile or two to cultural studies' movement away from its intellectual "roots," roots once firmly planted in the social and material . . . world. (xxvi)

chapter one

Dead in the
Water on the
Royal Duchess

At 3:00 p.m., two hours before the *Royal Duchess* was to sail from San Francisco to Alaska, Jorge Saramango, the cabin steward, slipped his card into the door of cabin C178 on the Caribe Deck, to bring a bowl of fruit that had been ordered a couple of hours earlier. As he entered the room, he saw the occupant of the room lying facedown on the bed, with a steak knife sticking out of his back.

"Jesus," he cried. "There's been . . . there's been a murder in one of my cabins."

He found himself trembling and dropped the bowl of fruit he was holding, which shattered when it fell to the floor. The fruit rolled around on the floor. He hastily gathered the shards of glass and the fruit and dumped everything in the cabin's wastepaper basket. Then he went to the phone and dialed the purser.

The assistant purser, who was at the desk, answered.

"Purser's office," she said.

"This is Jorge Saramango, the cabin steward for room C178," he said.

"Something terrible has happened. I just entered the cabin to bring a bowl of fruit that had been ordered . . . and I discovered a dead body—"

1

"Good lord," said the assistant purser.

"It's worse," replied Saramango. "He's been murdered!"

"Murdered?" said the assistant purser. "Murdered, you say. How do you know?"

"There's a steak knife sticking out of his back. He'd ordered a steak and some other things to eat when he got on the ship . . . and somebody's stuck the steak knife in his back."

"Don't do anything!" said the assistant purser. "Close the door and wait for security to come. I'll alert the purser. Don't let anyone in except someone from the staff."

"Yes," said Saramango.

The assistant purser called the purser.

"I've got some bad news for you," she said. "The steward for C178 discovered a dead body in the room . . . with a knife sticking out of his back. He's been murdered!"

"A murder, you say! Unbelievable," replied the purser. "I'll call security and inform the captain right away."

Agostino Lombordo, the captain, got to room C178 a couple of minutes before the head of security arrived. He found the steward, Saramango, slumped over in a chair, his hands over his eyes, white as a ghost.

"What a terrible thing," said the captain. "It must have been a big shock to you."

"Yes," replied Saramango.

"Take the rest of the day off . . . and try to compose yourself," he told Saramango. "Above all, don't say anything to anyone about this! Not a word! Nobody else must know because we don't want to panic the passengers. I've sent for the police, who should be arriving shortly. I imagine they'll find out who did it and clear the matter up quickly. Remember— don't say anything to anyone about what you've seen. Not even your best friends on the crew."

"Yes, sir," said Saramango, who left the room.

As he left, Jürgen Habermos, the chief of security, arrived.

"Damn," he said. "A murder. It's just beyond belief. This is all we need to complicate things. As if keeping an eye out for terrorists isn't enough!"

"The police should be here shortly," replied Lombordo. "Then we'll know what to do. It's a real mess. I've asked them not to bring uniformed officers on board. I don't want the passengers to know what has happened. If they found out it would be a disaster!"

A short while later there was a knock on the door. The captain opened it slightly. He saw a short man with a neatly trimmed beard. He was wearing a tweed Brooks Brothers suit, brown John Lobb shoes, a Silka striped tie, and a brown Borsalino hat. He had sparkling blue eyes and an animated expression on his face. Behind him was a tall, stooped man with a thin mustache, in a tan suit, and three other men. The man leading the procession held up his wallet, showing his credentials.

"Inspector Solomon Hunter," he said. "I'm here with my colleague Sergeant Weems and a team of our technicians. May we come in?"

"Of course," said the captain. "My name is Agostino Lombordo. . . . I am the captain of this ship. And this officer with me is our chief of security, Jürgen Habermos."

Hunter and his colleagues entered the room. He looked at the dead body on the bed and walked over to it. Then he scanned the room. It was as if he were taking a mental photograph. On a small desk he noticed a laptop computer and a camera. There were also several piles of papers and a number of books next to them. On a small table there was a tray with a large plate with the remains of a steak dinner on it, a fork and two teaspoons, three small plates, a half-empty coffee cup, and a water glass.

"Kind of cramped in here," Hunter said. "I'm going to have my men dust for fingerprints and take photos . . . that kind of thing. Can we go somewhere and talk while they do their work?"

"Of course," said the captain. "Come to my office."

"Give the place a thorough once-over," Hunter said to the technicians he had brought with him. "I want an inventory of everything you find in the cabin. Let me know what's in the computer and get the film in the camera developed. When you're done, bring the body to the station. . . . I want a complete autopsy as soon as possible."

He put on some latex gloves and took a wallet from the man's back pocket and opened it. He looked at the man's driver's license.

"We have here someone named Marshall McInnis," he said. "He's got some cards in one of the pockets of the wallet. Let's see if they shed more light on things."

He pulled out a card and read it.

"Professor Marshall McInnis, Amos Birdwhistell Chair of Media Studies, Annenberg School for Communication, University of Southern California."

"Don't tell me," said Weems. "Another academic. Why do they always have to kill one another in San Francisco?"

"That camera . . . we can have our photographers develop it for you right away," said Captain Lombordo. "If that would help your investigation."

"That will be fine," said Hunter. He examined the contents of the wallet and then put it in a plastic bag and gave it to one of his men.

"Keep this with all the other stuff you take," he said.

Lombordo led Hunter and Weems to an elevator, which they took to the top deck. He opened a door and led them up some stairs to the deck where the officers had their cabins, opened a door, and ushered them into his suite. He picked up a phone and said something in Italian.

"I've ordered some sandwiches, coffee, and pastries for you," he said. "In case you need something to eat. I've also asked the purser to get information about the occupants of that cabin, where we found the dead body. And I've made arrangements to have the film developed immediately."

"Thanks," said Hunter.

"There is a matter of some delicacy that I must speak to you about," added Lombordo. "The *Royal Duchess* is set to sail in less than an hour. There are 1,600 passengers on board and 700 crew members.

And, aside from the steward and the other members of the crew who were involved with notifying me, nobody else knows about the murder. Is it possible to have the body taken off on a freight gangplank so the passengers taking the cruise won't become aware of what has transpired? It might cause them to panic, and most certainly would cast a dark cloud over the cruise. As you might well imagine, many of the passengers have come great distances to take this cruise and for some it is a trip of a lifetime. I would like to make sure they have a happy experience."

"Yes, I understand," said Hunter. "That's not a problem. If anyone notices what's going on, we'll say he died of a heart attack, to give us some cover."

"Thank you, thank you so much," said the captain. Beads of perspiration were rolling down his forehead.

"I must make a phone call and arrange for that," he told Hunter. He picked up a cell phone and punched some numbers into it. Then he spoke with someone for a minute in Italian.

"My men can take the body off the ship from the freight gangplank. It doesn't make any difference to us," said Hunter.

"I can't thank you enough," said the captain.

"Is it possible that the murderer came on board, murdered McInnis, and then left the ship?" asked Hunter.

"Impossible," said Lombordo. "Due to security precautions, no guests are allowed on the ship. Everyone who boards the ship is photographed, and all their luggage is X-rayed. Unless the murderer found a way to get on board through the freight gangplank, kill his victim, and then get off again, all of which is highly unlikely, he is still on board. We have an officer guarding the freight gangplank, and nobody goes on the ship without a proper identification. The murderer . . . he's still on board. Of that I am certain."

"Or she," said Hunter. "Our murderer might be a woman."

"Yes . . . yes, of course," said Lombordo. "I know little of such things."

"If the murderer is still on board," said Hunter, "some of your other passengers may very well be in danger. If the murder wasn't random and just a chance occurrence, it means that the murderer may have other victims in mind. That's a problem we have to consider."

"I . . . I hadn't thought of that," replied Lombordo. He paused for a moment to think.

"The murderer could be a member of crew, couldn't he . . . or she?" said Weems.

"That's possible but very unlikely," replied the captain. "The members of the crew are very busy during boarding. A crew member might possibly steal something from a passenger's suitcase during the boarding period, and during cruises there are occasional rapes. But murder? Most improbable!

"Perhaps, and this may sound a bit odd," the captain added, "perhaps you and your colleague, Sergeant Weems, would like to continue your investigation during the cruise? We have an extra cabin, and you could search for the murderer while the *Royal Duchess* cruises to Alaska. You would be doing us a great favor if you accepted this invitation. Truly. As my guests, of course."

"Can't your security people on the ship handle this matter?" asked Weems. "I've got tickets for the Giants game tonight, and my wife has her heart set on going to the game."

"Talcott," said Hunter, "you've got to remember that there's a killer on board. We've got to do something, and there isn't time to get anyone else to handle the case."

"Sergeant Weems," said the captain, "if you and the inspector can help us with this matter, my company will get you tickets for a dozen games. And very good ones, too. Also for Inspector Hunter."

"He likes opera," said Weems.

"Very well, then," said the captain, "he will get some very fine opera tickets. You must realize that millions of dollars are riding on your decision. If the ship cannot sail or if the passengers find out about the murder, it will be a terrible blow to my company. A disaster!"

"OK," said Hunter. "We can't prevent the ship from sailing, and if it's going to sail with a murderer on board, it does make sense to have someone from our department on board, with experience in murder cases, searching for the killer."

The phone rang and the captain answered it.

"Yes," said Captain Lombordo. "Yes . . . yes," he replied. "Send the information up immediately."

He turned to Hunter.

"It seems the victim was part of a group of seven people. They all booked together from the same travel agent and are in adjoining state-rooms. I'll have the names for you shortly. They were put together in a table for ten. I'll arrange for you to dine at the same table with them. I'll have someone speak to the maître d' about that. We'll switch the people who had been assigned to dine with them. It can be managed quite easily."

"That should help," Hunter replied. "I'd appreciate it if you could provide me with their photographs as soon as possible. Now, if I can make a phone call in private, to check things out with the depart-ment brass, I can let you know whether we get permission to do this. I also want to have our researchers get some information on the people who were on the cruise with McInnis. We'll also ask for information from Interpol, to make sure we don't overlook anything."

"My private office is available to you," said the captain.

He got up and opened the door to his office.

"You can make your call here, in privacy," he said.

"Thanks," said Hunter, as he closed the door.

Hunter returned several minutes later.

"At first, the chief thought it was a practical joke. But when he found out what happened, he gave us permission. His secretary is going to call our wives and let them know why we'll be gone. It's highly un-usual to take a cruise and search for a murderer at the same time, but it does make sense."

"We will provide you with some clothes, toiletries, and all that, and you'll have an excellent stateroom—one with a large window, mind you."

"Thank you," said Hunter.

"Me, too," said Weems. "I've never been on a cruise before. This is kind of exciting."

The captain smiled. "No, it is I who thank you. You will have to be most circumspect in your investigation. If anyone discovers that the police are aboard conducting an official investigation, they will get curious and rumors will spread. If the word gets out, everyone will hear about it in just a few hours, at the most, and there will be chaos on board the ship. So the utmost discretion is called for."

"Of course," said Hunter. "We can keep our part of the bargain, but you must make sure the steward and the pursers don't say anything. The victim's colleagues will want to know what happened to him. Tell them that he died from a heart attack. I'd send each of them a note of condolence to prevent rumors from spreading. Make sure they get it after the ship has sailed."

"Yes, I will," said Captain Lombordo. "That's an excellent idea. We'll send some suitcases with clothes for you to wear on the cruise, so your steward will think you're regular passengers whose suitcases were sent to the wrong room. If you need anything else, just let me know," he said. "Just tell the purser, and he will arrange for anything you might need. I will arrange to have cards issued to you immediately for any purchases you might want to make—drinks, toiletries, things like that. Everything will be charged on my account, of course, though your names will be on the cards. We don't use money on the ship. It greatly simplifies things. You can always send messages to me through the purser or call my private number." He gave them his card and scribbled a phone number on it.

He picked up a phone and spoke with the purser for a few minutes.

"A steward will be here shortly to show you to your stateroom . . . room B242 on the Baja Deck. I can't thank you enough. So far, only the cabin steward who discovered the body, our chief of security, the assistant purser, the purser, and myself know about the murder. We will do all we can to make certain that nobody else finds out."

"You forgot one person who knows about the murder," said Hunter.

"Someone else?" asked the captain.

"Yes," said Hunter.

"And who would that be?" asked the captain.

"The murderer!" replied Hunter.

Marine architects now work with chefs and marketing executives to determine what the target market for a new ship will be and thus the menu is specially designed to please that market. Only once the food is selected are the galley size and the equipment needed determined—not before.

For instance, when Seabourn commissioned its two ships, its research showed that upscale travelers regarded the perceived quality of a line's cuisine as the single most important factor in the success or failure of the entire cruise. They recognized that all meals on this luxurious vessel would need to be true haute cuisine—or as they called it, "Nouvelle Classic." This style of food would be cooked to order—à la minute—and there would be many special orders that were not on the menu. Two more considerations at this point in the planning process were the amount of space that had been set aside for the galley and the number of crew available.

With this information factored in a menu plan was established. Each dinner menu would contain four appetizers (two hot, two cold), three soups (two hot, one cold), two salads, five entrees (one fish, one seafood, one roast, one grill, and one sauté), a cold seafood plate, and four desserts. Similar decisions were made for breakfast service (in-suite, restaurant, and verandah buffet), luncheon, 24-hour room service, tea service, and cocktail hour, and sample menus were developed for each of these. It was decided that for proper restaurant service the food would need to be plated in the kitchen to ensure quality and attractive presentation. (47)

Bob Dickson and Andy Vladimir, *Selling the Sea: An Inside Look at the Cruise Industry*

chapter **two**

Passing under the
Golden Gate Bridge

The cabin steward led them to their stateroom, gave them plastic key cards, and showed them how to use the safe.

"My name is Gilberto. I'm your cabin steward," he said. "The purser asked me to show you to your cabins. Your suitcases will be here shortly. I don't know why they aren't here already, but mix-ups do occur from time to time. I hope you enjoy your cruise. Please let me know if there's anything I can do for you."

With that, he left.

"What will we tell people if they ask what we're doing on the cruise?" asked Weems. "I've got to have something to tell people who ask."

"Yes, you're right," said Hunter. "Let's stay as close to the truth as possible. Let's tell people, if anyone asks, that we're civil servants for the city of San Francisco. You can say we were given the cruise as a gift. It's actually true."

"Okay," said Weems. "That works."

At 4:15 there was an emergency drill, which took half an hour or so. And then, at 5:00 p.m., they could feel the ship's engine throbbing as the *Royal Duchess* slipped away from the dock and started heading to sea.

"Let's go up on the top deck and see what the Golden Gate looks like from underneath," said Hunter. They left their cabin and walked up a number of flights of stairs to the Lido Deck, and then up another flight of stairs to the Sun Deck, where people were standing around drinking, watching a fire ship spray streams of water into the bay, and taking photographs. The sun was out and the sky was blue, and everyone seemed animated and excited. Waiters carrying trays with multicolored drinks in strangely shaped glasses were racing around, selling the drinks to passengers, who were using their ship credit cards for the first time.

Hunter and Weems watched as the *Royal Duchess* passed under the Golden Gate Bridge, with only six or eight feet to spare, from the top of its highest antenna.

"I've lived here for thirty years," said Weems, "and never got quite this close a view of the underside of the bridge. Never thought I would."

People were chatting and in very high spirits, as they watched San Francisco start to recede into the background. A band was playing on the deck below and some people were singing.

"It's very beautiful out on the ocean. . . . Let's enter into the spirit of it all," said Hunter. "Talcott . . . I'm going to treat you to a drink."

He motioned to a waiter, in a starched white coat, who was passing by with a tray full of drinks.

"Could you kindly tell me what that is?" he asked, pointing to a tall, bulbous glass filled with a pink liquid.

"A Tropical Fantasia, sir," replied the waiter.

"How does that sound, Talcott?" asked Hunter.

"I'm game," said Weems.

"Two Tropical Fantasias it is," said Hunter.

Hunter paid for the drinks with his card, and the waiter scurried off.

"To Captain Lombordo," he said softly, "who's paying for this. I hope he doesn't think we're taking advantage of his generosity."

"That's a laugh," said Weems. "If all the passengers scurried off the ship when we docked, or if they all cowered in their cabins, he'd be in a really lousy mood. No, he'll be very happy to pay for whatever we spend on tropical drinks or toothpaste or whatever."

"According to the captain there are something like 2,300 people on this ship, counting the passengers and crew," said Hunter. "And one of them has reason to be concerned, if not worried, that something went wrong. Perhaps more than one? Murderers always assume that they'll get away with their crimes, but they also worry that they might have made some little mistake that will lead to them being caught. Or that someone noticed something that will lead to their downfall. It's just about certain that someone on this ship killed McInnis. We've got to find that person. It's going to be a challenge, Talcott. Because this time we have to do everything on the sly. No official interrogations or anything like that."

"Maybe I should call you 'Hercules' or 'Sherlock,'" said Weems. "You'll be a consulting detective in the classical tradition, not a private eye like Sam Spade but one of those guys who never gets bopped on the head or anything like that, someone who just uses his little gray cells. Maybe Nero Wolfe?"

"But not as fat, certainly," said Hunter. "I'll be Holmes, and you can be my Dr. Watson. Why not? Something different for a change."

The *Royal Duchess* was now out of the bay and began to rock a bit in the open ocean. People started going below, where it wasn't so windy, and getting ready for their first day at sea.

"Let's go back to our cabin and see if there's some clothes for us and any messages," said Hunter. "I think it will be a good idea to sit at the table with the people who booked this cruise with our victim. After all, one of them, most likely, is the murderer."

When they returned to the cabin, they found a large envelope from the captain with maps of the ship and the ship's newspaper, *Duchess Daily*. The captain enclosed a letter that contained the names of the people who had booked the tour with McInnis and their photographs, which were taken when they boarded the ship. It also had a list of the academic institutions they were connected with.

"We've got quite a collection here," said Hunter. "It looks like they're from all over the place." He read their names: "Marshall McInnis, Symphonie Wu, Jean-Marie Benetton, Katarina Mittags, Antonia Fathom, Anastasia Lotman, and Sigfried Duerfklein. McInnis had his own cabin, C178, but the others are sharing cabins. Symphonie Wu and Anastasia Lotman are in C174 together, Katarina Mittags and Antonia Fathom are in C176, and Jean-Marie Benetton and Sigfried Duerfklein are in C180. So it looks like they were all next to one another."

The envelope also had a card indicating that they were at table 102 for the first sitting. Hunter looked at the letter and smiled.

"You're out of luck again, Talcott. Every one of the people who booked with McInnis is an academic."

"More murdering professors," replied Weems. "Damn! I thought the postmodernists were something until we ran into those mass communication theorists who killed one another off. God only knows what this bunch will be like."

"We'll discover that soon enough," said Hunter. "We'll be at their table, and that's for the first sitting at 6:00 p.m., in just a short while. So be prepared to make pleasant table talk while we try to find out as much as we can. Breakfasts and lunches are open seating, so it's only at dinner that you'll have to put up with them."

Weems looked at *Duchess Daily*.

"Get a load of this," he said. "There are a million things going on in this ship—gambling, dancing, art auctions, shows, massages—you name it. I can see that people who take cruises can keep busy. I'm going to keep my mouth shut most of the time and let you do the talking. That's the way we usually operate, anyway. I may eat at the buffet most evenings, to make life simpler for you. In fact, I think I'll do that tonight, if you don't mind."

"Not at all," said Hunter. "I understand, though, that on cruises the food is much better in the dining room than the buffet. You can have your breakfasts and lunches there, to see what it's like, if you don't want to eat with the professors.

"I'm off to start our investigation," said Hunter, looking at his watch. It was almost 6:00 p.m. He walked down the narrow passageway on which his cabin was located, then walked down a few flights of stairs until he reached the Promenade Deck, where the Palm Court dining room was located. It was filling up with people. A band of three musicians was playing music. He showed his card to one of the waiters at the entrance and was led to table 102. The other people at the table had already been seated and were talking in an animated manner with one another.

"Anastasia—don't you understand," said an elderly man, "that identity is, in essence, a function of the individual psyche, and that unconscious imperatives shape our behavior? When will you see the light?"

"There's no light in the unconscious, Sigfried," said a blonde woman who was arguing with him. "Freud was too simplistic, and his focus on the individual psyche poses problems in talking about people in general, I fear. With identity, it is perception that is all important, and, in particular, the various semiotic signifiers, which shape how we present ourselves to others, are what is basic! We're sign-sending and sign-interpreting animals!"

"But what about the influence of our culture and, in particular, of the postmodern mind-set that makes a shambles of all essentialist portrayals of identity?" said a man who was sitting near her. "There is no essence to identity, especially in postmodern times. It keeps changing and so does how we see it."

"Looks like a tablemate," said the elderly man, who noticed Solomon Hunter walking toward them. Everyone suddenly stopped arguing and gazed at Solomon Hunter intently.

"Good evening," Hunter said, introducing himself and smiling. "My name is Solomon Hunter. It seems that I've been assigned to this table. I'm on the cruise with a friend who'll be joining us tomorrow. He's going to try the buffet tonight." Hunter sat down at the table, which was located near a large window. "My friend's somewhat antisocial, if you know what I mean."

He took a seat between a Chinese woman and an older gentleman with a short white beard.

"Pleased to meet you," said the Chinese woman. She was a very pretty woman in her late thirties, with long black hair that fell to her shoulders. She had a lovely smile. "My name is Symphonie Wu. I'm a professor from the Beijing Broadcasting Institute. I'm a media scholar . . . interested in how the media affect large numbers of people. I'll allow my friends at the table to introduce themselves. We're all professors. I hope that won't intimidate you." She laughed.

"My name is Anastasia Lotman," said a beautiful woman of about thirty, with wavy blonde hair and sparkling green eyes. "I work in a field of communication known as semiotics in Italy." There was a kind of self-confidence about her that struck Hunter's attention.

"I'm Jean-Marie Benetton," said the person next to her. He was a man in his midforties, who seemed rather surprised by Solomon's arrival at their table. "I'm a sociologist from France doing research on postmodernism. This year I'm visiting at Harvard University."

"That's a subject I find quite interesting and very puzzling," said Hunter.

"You know about postmodernism?" said Benetton, in a surprised tone. "Most people in the United States don't."

"Yes," replied Hunter. "By chance I've had the pleasure of meeting a number of postmodernists over the years. They seem to be a dime a dozen in San Francisco."

"The Berkeley connection, of course," said Benetton. "Until his death a few years ago, Ettore Gnocchi, one of the most important postmodernist thinkers, taught at Berkeley. I admired his work a great deal."

"I'm Katarina Mittags," said the woman seated next to him. She had short, mousy-blonde hair that looked as if it had been dyed and spoke with a slight German accent. There was a look of intensity and determination on her face.

"My name is Antonia Fathom," said a redheaded woman with short hair who was seated next to Katarina. "I'm a linguistics professor and a feminist from Britain, out exploring the Wild West of America . . . looking for signs of civilization." She had an upper-class English accent and, Hunter noted, a sense of humor. "Are linguists a dime a dozen in San Francisco as well?"

Hunter laughed.

"I am Sigfried Duerfklein," said the last person of the group. He was a short man in his late sixties or early seventies with a white beard and round, black-rimmed glasses. "I'm a psychiatrist from the University of Vienna. I'm interested in the relationship between the psyche and identity. We're all interested in exploring different facets of identity. It is, we all believe, one of the central problems of the age. It was a topic that was of great interest to Freud and many other important thinkers of his time."

"How interesting. I'm sure I'll learn a great deal about identity, and many other things, from having dinner with you each evening. I look forward to it a great deal," said Hunter.

"You must excuse us if we're a bit glum tonight," said Symphonie. "We've just had some terrible news. The captain of the ship sent us notes to the effect that one of our party, Marshall McInnis, died suddenly from a heart attack while we were in port. He was leading the identity project that we're all working on. You can imagine how shocking that information was. We were expecting a happy and productive ten days, but shortly after we sailed away from San Francisco we learned about our friend's death. But we'll do what we can to salvage the project and enjoy the cruise."

"I'm sorry to hear that," said Hunter.

"Yes, we'll do what we can," said Katarina, "but the timing was terrible. Our colleague, Marshall McInnis, was so full of life and so vital that it doesn't seem possible that he's dead. It is a terrible shock and a loss to all of us. And to sociology. He was one of the leading sociologists of the day, an expert on media and communications and one of the pioneers in our field—cultural studies."

"You should understand that this cruise was to be a working vacation for us," said Jean-Marie Benetton. "We're all scholars and researchers, all from different universities all over the world, most of us visiting professors this year at various institutions here and there in America. Our plan was that during the cruise each of us would write a chapter on the area of research that we specialize in, for a cultural studies book on the problem of identity. The idea was that each of us would work on his or her chapter a bit each day and have a chapter done by the end of the cruise. But now I don't know. I don't know if I can put my mind to it now."

"I think we still should," said Antonia Fathom. "We must. It will help us keep our minds off of Marshall's death and will be a kind of tribute to him. I think we should carry on."

"I agree," said Katarina. "If Marshall already wrote his chapter, we will use it. If not, we must find someone else to write it. But we should not lose this opportunity to write a book that will be of use to scholars and students and others, that will—if I may be so bold—revolutionize the cultural studies approach to identity."

"You'll hear that word from Katarina often," said Symphonie. "Antonia may have red hair, but Katarina is the real Red in the group."

At this everyone laughed, but in a restrained, almost pained way.

"Antonia likes to kid me about my Marxism," said Katarina. "I'm used to it. But tell me," she added, turning to Hunter, "are you, by chance, a scholar? All of us at the table are professors, and I can only wonder whether the gods of chance have sent another one here to us. If you don't mind my saying so, you look like a scholar. Perhaps even a dean or maybe a college president." She scrutinized Hunter as she spoke. "Yes, from the way you're dressed and the way your carry yourself I'd say very much a college president."

Hunter laughed.

"No, I'm afraid not," he replied. "But curiously enough I've had a good deal to do with professors and academic types over the years. I'm just a humble civil servant for the city of San Francisco. And so is my friend. One way or another, though, we've had lots of experiences with professors. We have quite a few universities in the city, you know."

Everyone at the table started looking at Hunter carefully. As they chatted, they were all busy trying to figure out who Solomon Hunter was, what he was like, and what he did. He had a neatly trimmed gray beard and was beautifully dressed. There was something about his face that puzzled the people around the table. He had bright, twinkling blue eyes and a curious expression of bemusement on his face. And yet, you could not help but notice that he listened carefully to anything that was said and took everything in. You had the feeling that he saw everything, remembered everything, and yet, remarkably, he gave nothing away about himself or what he was observing.

"We are pleased to have such an interesting tablemate," said Symphonie. "I can sense, right away, that we're really fortunate in having you at our table. I understand that some tablemates are really terrible and can ruin a cruise. I can see you're different. We don't spend much time with civil servants in our jobs, so this will be an opportunity for us to get a different perspective on things. Too bad you don't know anything about the humanities and about social science methods and our general field—cultural studies."

Hunter looked at the people sitting around the table. They looked like any other group of people sitting around a table, and yet, it was quite likely that one of these people was a murderer. But which one?

"Thank you, you're most kind," replied Hunter. "Over the years, by chance, of course, I've had the opportunity to meet quite a few professors. I got my degree from the University of California in Berkeley, and since I've worked in San Francisco for many years, I've had dealings with a number of academics, in fields such as literary criticism, media theory, and postmodernism, among other things. I guess, from what you've told me so far, that my experience with all these professors counts as being a rough approximation of cultural studies."

"Tell me," asked Sigfried. "Were your encounters of educational benefit?"

"Most certainly," said Hunter. "I learned a great deal. You always do when you hang around professors. That's what I've found."

The waiter appeared and handed menus to everyone. "My name is Alberto," he said. "I'm your waiter. And this," he said, pointing to a young man who looked to be in his midtwenties, "is your assistant waiter, Marcos."

At this, Marcos nodded and smiled.

Hunter looked at the menu. There were seven courses and five or six choices for each course, plus dessert. It was mind-boggling.

"Alberto," said Hunter, "what do you recommend?"

"The filet mignon is excellent," he said. "I'd start with a shrimp cocktail. The lobster bisque is very good, as are the gnocchi. We always have a pasta course for the evening meal. I can order a half serving, if anyone would like to try our pasta course. Now, as for your salads . . ."

It took a while for everyone to order dinner. There were seven courses, and people chose different things for most of the courses, though Hunter noticed that everyone at the table ordered the filet mignon. And they all ordered their steaks rare.

As soon as the child begins to move about and explore, he begins to ponder the problem of his identity. When he spies his mirror image, he wonders whether what he sees is really he, or a child just like him standing behind this glassy wall. He tries to find out by exploring whether this other child is really, in all ways, like him. He makes faces, turns this way or that, walks away from the mirror and jumps back in front of it to ascertain whether this other one has moved away or is still there. Though only three years old, the child is already up against the difficult problem of personal identity.

The child asks himself: "Who am I? Where did I come from? How did the world come into being? Who created man and all the animals? What is the purpose of life?" True, he ponders these vital questions not in the abstract, but mainly as they pertain to him. He worries not whether there is justice for individual man, but whether *he* will be treated justly. He wonders who or what projects him into adversity, and what can prevent this from happening to him. Are there benevolent powers? How should he form himself and why? Why has all this happened to him? What will it mean for his future? Fairy tales provide answers to these pressing questions, many of which the child becomes aware of only as he follows the stories. (47)

Bruno Bettelheim, *The Uses of Enchantment: The Meaning and Importance of Fairy Tales*

chapter **three**

CURIOUSLY ENOUGH, I'VE HAD A GOOD DEAL TO DO WITH PROFESSORS OVER THE YEARS...

The Identity Problem

"So tell me," Hunter asked, as they were eating their shrimp cocktails, "what are you going to write about in this book on identity? How come it's of interest to you? I'm not an academic, so I don't know what the latest hot topics are in universities. I know there was a postmodernism boom that lasted for a while, but I take it that it has faded away."

"Not entirely," said Jean-Marie Benetton. He was a man of about forty, with light brown hair. He projected a sense of assurance and self-confidence. "There is still a great deal of interest in postmodernism, which you can tell by looking at the number of books that are being published on the subject. There are some, of course, who argue that we are now in a post-postmodern era, whatever it might be called. We at the CNRS—that's the National Center for Scientific Research in France—are doing a great deal of work on the matter of postmodernism. My particular interest is in how it relates to identity. One important postmodern theorist, Jean Baudrillard, said that whoever lives by meaning dies by meaning, which suggests, in effect, that in the postmodern world, meaning has disappeared. And if it has disappeared, so has the significance of identity. An American postmodernist, Fredric Jameson, has also dealt with the subject."

"Identity," said Katarina Mittags, "is a site for contestation in the academy. Is it essentially tied to psychological matters, as our colleague Sigfried and his master Freud would argue? A psychoanalyst, Erik Erikson, wrote a book called *Identity: Youth and Crisis*, around forty years ago, that attracted a great deal of attention to the subject of identity and really got the ball rolling, as you Americans would say. On the other hand, sociologists in the twenties, such as Charles Horton Cooley, argued that identity is socially constructed, with what he called a 'looking-glass self,' which means that others are involved in our developing a sense of identity. Another sociologist of about the same time period, George Herbert Mead, talked about 'significant others' who help us establish our identity. For such sociologists, self and society are two sides of the same coin. Individuals, in a sense, are created by society."

"That's fairly close to Saussure's argument that signs are made of signifiers and signifieds," said Anastasia. "He would see identity as connected to the signs we send others about ourselves and the way they receive them. A French semiotician, Roland Barthes, has dealt with French identity in his book *Mythologies*. In many respects, their insistence of the role of culture in generating and helping people to interpret signs puts them close to the theories of Cooley or Mead."

"Yes," said Katarina. "That's a good point. There are other considerations that scholars interested in identity investigate, such as gender, which Antonia believes is crucial; or race, which Symphonie's work focuses on; or class and occupation, as I've argued; or the media and popular culture, that poor Marshall worked on. You see, there's no agreement about what is fundamental in determining identity. That's why it is such an important topic and one best dealt with from a cultural studies approach. Cultural studies itself has changed. Originally, when it developed at the University of Birmingham in England, it was quite radical and obsessed with class and power, but in recent years it has broadened its approach and now deals with many other matters."

"We've taken the ideological fixation out of cultural studies," said Sigfried. "We've tamed the beast."

"Some of us," added Symphonie, "combine different approaches. For example, my interest in race is connected to the problem of representation, which one of the Birmingham scholars, Stuart Hall, has worked on. He has written about how representation is connected to the way people think about race, drawing on semiotics, communication theory, and other disciplines."

"There's not even any agreement on what identity is," said Antonia. "What do you think it is, Solomon? With a name like yours, we expect you have some very wise insights to offer us!"

"Do you expect me to answer that question, after what you've just told me about the difficulties in dealing with the subject?" said Solomon.

"But a layman's view may be of interest," said Anastasia. She had a slight Russian accent. "You need not be afraid of us. We won't bite you, not when there's so much wonderful food to eat on this ship."

"I must confess," Hunter replied, "that I never thought about it much, but I would say that for most people identity means who you are, where you live, what you do, and what you're like. That kind of thing. I know that answer's rather vague."

"Yes," said Sigfried, "but how do people become who they are? And what does 'who you are' mean? Is it your race, your religion, your occupation, your social class, your personality, your gender, your culture, your politics, or some combination of all of these, and if so, which of these matters is most important? Or are they all equally important? That's what we're investigating. How does a person become whomever or whatever he or she becomes? How do we arrive at ourselves? How long does it last? And what role does society play in our identities? An early sociologist, Gustave Le Bon, argued in his book *The Crowd* that we lose our identities in crowds. He influenced early American sociologists and even more contemporary thinkers who dealt with identity, such as Erich Fromm. I think Marshall McInnis and others like him who work on the media and popular culture were also influenced by him."

Sigfried had only the slightest touch of a German accent.

"I suggest we let poor Solomon eat his dinner in peace and stop pestering him," said Symphonie. "He's on this cruise to relax and not to be caught up in a dinner table seminar on conflicting approaches to identity."

"Thanks, Symphonie," said Hunter, "but you've all aroused my curiosity, and now, I confess, I find that the problem of identity has become quite interesting to me. You've all turned me on to the subject, and I realize that, in a way, I've been concerned with it myself for a number of years, though I never recognized it. So don't let me interfere with your work and your discussions. I find it much better than chitchat about the weather or the kind of conversations one has about subjects of no importance at parties and other social gatherings. If, for one reason or another, you don't wish to talk about your work on identity at the dinner table, I hope each of you will tell me about your work over a drink or while taking a promenade around the ship. Or at breakfast or lunch, when there's no reserved seating."

"That sounds fine," said Antonia. "I have an intuition that you were, somehow, fated to be at our table, though I can't say exactly why I feel the way I do. Was it just a matter of chance or something else? I'm sure, of course, that you know a great deal more than you let on. Too bad that Marshall didn't have the chance to meet you. I think you'd have got on well with him and would have found him a most stimulating person."

"What was he like?" asked Hunter.

"He was brilliant, charming, but also infuriating," said Symphonie. "I was married to him for a few months a number of years ago. We met in the summer, had what you'd call a 'whirlwind' romance, and ran off to Las Vegas to get married. It only took a short while for the bloom to fade from the rose, and I realized that I had made a terrible mistake. So we got a quick divorce. It was all quite amicable, fortunately. I loved him, but I simply couldn't stand living with him. With Marshall, you never could tell what he was thinking. When you had a conversation with him, you always had the feeling his mind was working desperately to find a good pun to interject in the conversation or that his mind was somewhere else, perhaps in the thirteenth century, thinking about something vaguely connected to the subject of your conversation. I also discovered that he believed in what he called an open marriage. He wanted to be able to have sex with anyone he could lure into bed with him. I found out about this, alas, after we had married. The situation was quite intolerable, so we split up as quickly as we had got together. But we were still friends."

"Hmm," thought Hunter. "Sounds like a satyromaniac or sexual predator. Just the kind of person to make a lot of enemies, especially of angry husbands or bitter women who have been cast off."

"Symphonie knew him better than anyone else around the table, having been married to him," said Anastasia. "We only knew his 'social self,' and in public he was witty, charming, and full of interesting and sometimes wild ideas. He was always on good behavior at conferences and when giving guest lectures, though there was a good deal of gossip about his chasing about after young graduate students. But he wasn't different from many other professors in that respect, if you think about it."

"So I understand," said Hunter.

"Marshall was, despite his problems, a lovely man," said Symphonie. "But I found him simply impossible to live with. Maybe I had unrealistic notions about what marriage would be like. He would have said I was a victim of our pop-culture delusions, that I had a mass-mediated mentality and believed in all kinds of silly things that advertising agencies had put into my head. He had been a philosopher, but he became interested in the mass media and popular culture. He believed that we all have mass-mediated minds, that our beliefs and values have been shaped, in important ways, by the mass media and pop culture. That's why he brought us all together, to see how people arrive at their identities. We still don't know how people become themselves. It remains a mystery."

"I love mysteries," said Solomon. "More than you can possibly imagine. Not only the kind written by Agatha Christie but the kind you're talking about. That is, I'm very curious about why people behave the way they do, and about how they get their identities or hide them. Now that you mention it, I can see that I've always been extremely interested in identity, though I never realized it, or would have put it the way all of you do."

"You have the makings of a good cultural studies scholar," said Sigfried. "I'm a psychiatrist and psychotherapist and have some ideas about what motivates people and how they become who and what they are. In a sense you could say that Marshall didn't take human consciousness into account. He thought that people, of all ages, mind you, were shaped by their experiences, and that since the average person spends a great deal of time watching television and listening to the radio and now playing video games, I could go on and on . . . he thought that these mass-mediated experiences led to their formation. You could say that he believed that information, from peers and parents, but mostly from pop culture, led to a person's formation—his or her belief structure, as well as values and personality. He thought that the media educated people, but that this education was primarily shaped by advertising, both directly, in terms of creating consumer lust, and also indirectly—he thought that advertising profoundly affected the content of television and other media as well. I think he was right, but Marshall discounted the fact that human beings have an unconscious, that they are profoundly affected by certain powerful drives and unconscious psychological imperatives that shape their behavior."

"The problem with Sigfried's psychoanalytic perspective," said Jean-Marie, "is that, like all Freudians, he discounts the importance of social forces. Freud did write about sociological matters, but they were always subservient to drives and various internal conflicts in the individual psyche. He was too deterministic. He put too much emphasis on childhood sexuality and the Oedipus complex and didn't recognize the ability of people to change when they were older . . . or be affected, in profound ways, by groups and other social and political phenomena.

"Another thing to keep in mind," said Jean-Marie, "is that our mental processes are shaped and mediated by language, and language is social, which means that mental processes are necessarily social. Psycho-analytic theorists don't take this into account. Of course Freud is passé now and has been for ages. . . ."

Alberto suddenly appeared with the dessert menu. Marcos had brought all the courses and Alberto had served everyone. He had learned, over the years, how to be attentive yet unobtrusive. He smiled when people spoke to him and answered all questions addressed to him about the dishes on the menu in detail. He was always correct about what the best things on the menu were, too.

"I hope you enjoyed your dinner. Was the filet mignon to your satisfaction?" asked Alberto.

"Quite fine," said Antonia. "I don't know how you serve such fine food to so many people." The others at the table murmured their agreement with Antonia's statement.

Alberto smiled.

"We have a hundred cooks," he said. "And they've had a lot of practice."

"What do you recommend for the desserts?" asked Solomon.

"The hazelnut chocolate soufflé with Armagnac cream is excellent. For those who don't want something as rich, the caramelized puff pastry pear tart is fine. It goes well with vanilla ice cream."

Everyone told Alberto what they wanted for dessert.

"I'd like a decaffeinated cappuccino with my dessert," said Hunter.

"I didn't know they had cappuccinos on the ship. I'll have one too," said Anastasia.

It turned out that everyone at the table decided to order a cappuccino, and Marcos went scurrying off to fetch the desserts and the coffee.

Alberto scraped the crumbs off the table with a metal crumb scraper. Marcos arrived with the coffee and the desserts. The soufflés were in small crocks and smelled wonderful.

"I'll have to go to the gym and spend hours there to work off this meal," said Katarina. "I don't want to think about how many calories we've eaten at this dinner."

Antonia glanced at her watch.

"I can't believe it. We've been here for almost two hours. This is absolutely incredible. The time just disappeared."

"Yes," said Sigfried, "but remember, you've just eaten a six-course meal, or was it seven? In any case, if you keep away from the rich desserts and do a lot of walking, I'm sure you'll survive this cruise without doing too much damage to your waistline. Just remember—a minute on the lips and a lifetime on the hips. That's what one of my students who worked in a gym once taught me. She gave me that line!"

He laughed.

"I hope you're right," said Antonia.

"I have to worry, also," said Jean-Marie. "When you get older, it seems to be a lot easier to put on the pounds than to take them off. I know I have to be careful, but it's so difficult to resist these fantastic meals."

"I read in one of the tour books that you shouldn't take the elevators," said Symphonie, "and that walking up and down the stairs and along the corridors of this ship will help you avoid gaining weight. And if you take long walks around the cities we're docking at, you should be fine. A friend of mine took this cruise and actually lost a couple of pounds. It's easy, I've been told, to walk from the ship to the center of Victoria. That's what I'm going to do when we get there."

"Lost weight on a cruise? That's hard to believe," said Katarina. "But something to hope for."

"There's a show on in twenty minutes in the theater. Does anyone want to go to see it with me?" asked Antonia. "I could use a bit of entertainment. It might help me digest the soufflé."

Everyone except Solomon and Anastasia, who said she didn't feel like going to a show, went off to see the show.

"Would you like to take a walk around the ship?" Solomon asked Anastasia. "We can become explorers! These cruise ships are quite enormous, and there are many interesting things to see on them."

"That would be very nice," replied Anastasia.

Douglas M. Kellner and Meenakshi Gigi Durham, "Adventures in Media and Cultural Studies: Introducing KeyWorks"

Geoffrey Gorer and John Rickman, *The People of Great Russia: A Psychological Study*

From the beginning, British cultural studies systematically rejected high/low culture distinctions and took media culture seriously, thus surpassing the elitism of the dominant literary approaches to culture. Likewise, British cultural studies overcame the limitations of the Frankfurt School notion of a passive and manipulated audience in their conceptions of an active audience that creates meanings and the popular. Reproducing the activism of oppositional groups in the 1960s and 1970s, the Birmingham School was engaged in a project aimed at a comprehensive criticism of the present configuration of culture and society, attempting to link culture and society, attempting to link theory and practice to orient cultural studies with a theory of social production and reproduction, specifying the ways that cultural forms served either to further social control, or to enable people to resist. It analyzed society as a hierarchical and antagonistic set of social relations characterized by the oppression of the subordinate class, gender, race, ethnic, and national strata. (16)

What Russians value are not minimum gratifications—enough to get along with—but maximum total gratifications—orgiastic feasts, prolonged drinking bouts, high frequency of copulations, and so on. Nearly all Russians would seem to prefer a huge feast, followed by months of meagre fare, rather than a little improvement in their daily diet. These preferences were institutionalized in the religious observances of peasant Russia: the prolonged ritual fasts and Gargantuan feasts with which Christmas and especially Easter were celebrated. (139)

chapter **four**

ANASTASIA LOTMAN
HAD LONG BLONDE HAIR
AND SPARKLING GREEN EYES

Anastasia Lotman

Anastasia and Solomon started wandering around the *Royal Duchess*.

"This ship has something like a dozen decks, but most of the interesting parts of it are on the top few decks," said Solomon. "Let's go out on the top deck, where we can get some fresh air . . . and work off that meal."

They started walking up stairs and finally arrived at the Sun Deck. There were a few other passengers wandering around the deck. The sea was calm now, and the ship was gliding through the water.

"It's very kind of you to keep me company," said Anastasia. "I'm generally a very social animal, but somehow, after Marshall's death, I don't feel like watching a show. Not that I liked him. In fact, I despised him. But still, the poor man died. We shouldn't think badly of the dead."

"Despised him?" repeated Solomon.

"Yes. He was a sexual predator who preyed on his students and anyone else he could lure into bed with him. He became very assertive one evening when we had been out drinking, but he didn't realize that I am a very strong woman."

"You don't look strong," said Solomon.

"I studied ballet for a dozen years and hoped to become a ballerina. Ballet dancers are all very strong. Most people don't know that. But

I had this growth spurt and became too tall to be a first-class ballerina. The male ballet dancers like petite little nothings to lift. Dancers are all egomaniacs. But the worst of them can't compare to professors."

Anastasia was a very beautiful woman. She was around five feet eight inches, was slender, and had long curly blonde hair and brilliant green eyes. She was wearing a green turtleneck jersey and some rather tight, form-fitting blue slacks.

"As you know," she said, "each of us is supposed to write a chapter for a book on the question of identity. There are, as we explained at dinner, many ways to look at the subject, but each of us thinks his or her way is really the most important way, and that the others all are of secondary importance. You're not a professor, so you probably don't realize that we all think the universe revolves around our discipline and our particular aspect of our disciplines, or maybe subdiscipline would be the way to put it. Universities are like medieval fiefdoms, full of self-important and often pompous snits. Little princes and princesses, prima donnas who think that what they are doing is of monumental importance, or try to convince themselves that such is the case, to be more precise."

"Kind of makes me glad I didn't become a professor," said Hunter. "I recall reading something that a former American senator, William Fulbright, once said. He explained that people become attached to ideologies and movements and that kind of thing to prevent themselves from facing the fact that their lives are really minor events in the ongoing universe. Maybe that explains why professors act the way they do."

"Senator Fulbright was a very wise man. I had a Fulbright scholarship and spent a year in the United States when I was much younger. I had a wonderful time," said Anastasia. "I was able to pursue my research on the semiotics of identity. A few years later, I got a job in Bologna, at the university there. It has a large semiotics program."

"And how does semiotics relate to identity?" asked Hunter. "I'm not sure what identity is, and I don't know very much about semiotics. I learned something about it a few years ago when I met a French professor who explained to me that semiotics is all about signs."

"Yes, signs. That's the key concept for semioticians. And for semioticians such as myself, it has to do with the way we use signs to create an identity for ourselves and make that identity more secure. Signs have two parts. You can think of signs as being two sides of a coin. One side is an object or sound, what one theorist called a 'signifier,' and the other side is the concept or idea that you get from the signifier. But the relation between the two is based on social conventions and subject to change."

"Does that mean that identities are never secure?" asked Hunter.

"Of course. You can think of an identity as a process with many different changes possible. A person manufactures his or her identity and secures it on the basis of how others react to that identity. If one identity doesn't work, it is possible to have a 'makeover' and try others. There is, you can see, a social aspect to identity. We create and re-create our identities based on a variety of things, such as our personalities and interests, but we are also dependent on others to interpret the signs we send correctly . . . and favorably."

"I see," said Hunter.

"Take me, for example," said Anastasia. "What do you think are the most important aspects of my identity? If someone saw you walking with me and later asked you about me, what would you tell them?"

Anastasia smiled.

"Well," said Hunter. "I'd tell them that you are a professor who is doing research on the semiotics of identity—whatever that might mean. That you are from Russia or one of the eastern European countries—judging from your name and your accent—and that you teach in a university in Bologna."

"Nothing else?" asked Anastasia.

"I might add that you are very pretty, have lovely green eyes, and very long, blonde hair," said Hunter.

"At last," said Anastasia. "You mention that I am a blonde. Most men would put it first. And that is because blonde hair is a very important signifier or identity marker. I'm a blonde. But am I really a blonde or am I dyeing my hair? Am I a bottle blonde?"

"Does it matter?" asked Hunter.

"Yes, it does," said Anastasia. "I happen to be a natural blonde, but many women dye their hair blonde because they want to take advantage of what blondeness means to most people, especially men. But a brunette or redhead or a woman with black hair who becomes a blonde brings a different personality and mentality to this state from the one that natural blondes have. A woman who dyes her hair blonde can be a blonde on the outside, but inside, she's still a brunette or whatever. Can you understand that?"

They were slowly circling the ship, and Hunter was enjoying the fresh air and the conversation.

"I think I understand what you're getting at. It's like the saying we have, 'You can take the boy out of Brooklyn, but you can't take the Brooklyn out of the boy.' Same kind of thing."

"And a very perceptive comment relative to the problem of identity, especially if the boy has a Brooklyn accent," replied Anastasia. "So you can see how some things—hair, in my case, and an accent, in terms of your Brooklyner—how signs can play a role in determining a person's identity. Remember that I said that the meanings of signs are based on conventions. If I were in my classroom in Bologna, I'd say that blonde hair is a signifier but that what is signified by blonde hair is open to interpretation. Tell me, Solomon, what does blondeness mean to you?"

"Blondes? When I think of blondes I think of Marilyn Monroe, and glamour and excitement. Having fun . . . that kind of thing."

"But aren't blondes also connected with innocence and purity? Many dolls for children have blonde hair. Could there also be something cold and asexual about blonde hair? D. H. Lawrence pointed out that in American novels blonde women tend to be cool and unobtainable, while women with dark hair are connected to sexiness and passion. So that raises an interesting problem for semioticians like myself. Let's take women with dark hair who dye their hair blonde. They are, in a sense, lying about their hair color but unintentionally telling the truth about their sexuality, that they are cold.

"All of this," she added, "is connected to primal attitudes human beings have towards light and darkness being equated with good and evil. So you can see, blonde hair is a very complicated signifier."

"So how do men make sense of all this? What do they see when they see a blonde, or do different men see blondes in different ways?" asked Hunter.

"If you grow up in a country where many women are naturally blonde, being blonde doesn't mean anything. But if you grow up in a country where everyone has dark hair and a dark complexion, then the classic blue-eyed honey blonde means something else. Some scholars have suggested that men of color in Middle Eastern and African countries lust after blondes as 'unobtainable' goddess figures, and when they come to countries like England and the Scandinavian countries, where there are many blondes, these men go wild. We always seek the other because, in a sense, it is 'the other' who helps confirm our identity.

"One of the founding fathers of semiotics, a Swiss linguist named Ferdinand de Saussure, said that concepts are differential and are defined not by their positive content but negatively, in terms of their relationship with other terms in the system. He said, 'In language there are only differences.' It is the nature of language, then, that shapes our thinking. And concepts have meaning by being the opposite of something, by being, as he would put it, what others are not. So we're always searching for what might be called oppositional 'others' to help us understand better who we are."

"Sort of 7 UP as the uncola kind of thing?" asked Hunter.

"Exactly. We make sense of the world by seeing things in terms of oppositions. Rich and poor, strong and weak, blonde and brunette."

"So—have dark-skinned men lusted after you?" asked Hunter. "You're an 'other,' and you're a real blonde to boot."

"That wouldn't matter to people who lust after blondes. It is the blonde hair color that is crucial—and the other signifiers that go with it, a light complexion, blue eyes if possible, and so on. But it turns out that after my divorce I married another blond, from Tartu, where I studied. We will help replenish the world's stock of natural blondes.

"What you have to realize," Anastasia added, "is that people are always sending messages to one another whether they are aware of this or not. And semiotics is the science that studies how these messages convey meaning. Not only is hair color a message, but so is hairstyle. Being a blonde with short hair is different from being one with long, wavy hair like mine. And then there are many other things that confer identity on people in addition to their use of language, such as the style of their glasses, their jewelry, their use of makeup, their body piercings, the clothes they wear, their body language. I could go on and on. An American sociologist, Orrin Klapp, wrote an interesting book about these matters—*The Collective Search for Identity*. It considers how people use signs to create identities, in many cases false identities.

"These items are messages about who you are or who you think you are or who you are trying to be, and the responses you get from others either suggest that your messages aren't getting through and people are confused about who you are, or they confirm your identity. So we semioticians who study identity are interested in how people create an identity for themselves through verbal and nonverbal means, recognizing that people often change their identities or lie about their identities. Umberto Eco, an Italian semiotician, said that if signs can tell the truth, they can also be used to lie. Blondes who dye their hair are, you can say, lying about their identity. So the semiotics of identity is a very interesting and complicated matter."

"Tell me, how did you get connected with Marshall McInnis? Did he lust for blondes, like just about everyone else?" asked Hunter, laughing.

"I had published a book, *Markers: The Semiotics of Identity*, that he liked," replied Anastasia. "I also had met him at various conferences.

He was invited to talk at many different conferences, all over the world, so it turned out we kept bumping into one another all over the world."

"An interesting choice of language," thought Hunter.

"What was his take on the identity question?" he asked.

"Marshall was interested in communication and media. Like all communications scholars, he thought that it was the central subject of the day, that everything involved communication and that the media played a big role in every aspect of life—especially in terms of shaping, or, rather, helping shape, an individual's identity. He always said that the media and pop culture—especially advertising and pop music—were raising our kids, so it shouldn't surprise us if they turned out different from the way we thought they would since they were, in a sense, strangers. He had analyzed advertising and other kinds of pop culture, and that led him on to theoretical matters. But despite his interest in theories of media, he was always concerned with how the media affected individuals and societies. He argued that we often identified with the pop-culture stars we saw and that if we couldn't imitate their lives, we could, at least, imitate their consumption patterns. Some scholars call this phenomenon 'mimetic desire,' imitating the desire of others. Poor Marshall. His death was a great loss. He was, you should realize, one of the founding fathers of cultural studies . . . and I would say a brilliant semiotician, though he didn't identify himself as such. He'll be missed."

"What about the others at our table? Do you think they feel the same way about him? Symphonie seemed to suggest there was a rather somber or dark side to him."

"I wasn't married to him, so I can't tell. I only saw his 'good,' or what Symphonie described as his 'social,' side. But I can imagine that like many powerful and famous men, he made any number of enemies. You have to realize that most professors in the United States don't do much in the way of contributing to knowledge; perhaps only 10 percent do most of the work in any discipline. The rest teach and help run their universities and get ahead that way. They might write an article or two or a textbook, but for the most part they just teach—not that teaching isn't important—and serve on countless committees. They tend to resent people like Marshall, who are so full of ideas and spirit, and who attract so much attention. I'm sure that Marshall made many scholars feel petty and irrelevant.

"Academics are terribly jealous, you know, even if they don't say anything that would indicate how they feel. In their departments they seek to hire others like them, who will not challenge them or make them feel inconsequential. So there is a kind of unsaid and probably unconscious conspiracy of these professors to choose second-rate scholars in their new hires. This is not always the case, and certainly not always the case in our first-tier universities, though a lot of first-class universities have deadwood in them, too. But you have to know that there are only a hundred or so really first-rate, selective universities in the United States. There are, of course, many wonderful teachers who don't advance scholarship, and their role is important. But people who earn doctorates are all trained to advance knowledge, and those who don't often have both an unconscious self-loathing and lingering resentments about those who do. I'm afraid that's a rather long-winded digression."

"No, not at all," said Solomon. "I'm not an academic and don't know much about such things. But what about professors in other countries? You teach in Italy. Does that apply to Italian universities?"

Anastasia laughed.

"You have to realize that in most universities outside of the United States there are hardly any professors, relatively speaking. You might have a department with a thousand students and two or three professors with chairs; the rest of the teaching is done by adjuncts, who hope, one day, to get a position in the university or who use their affiliation with the university for their own purposes. It isn't unusual to find a professor who lives in Rome or Milan and has a position in Bologna or who lives in Munich and teaches in Düsseldorf; that's because full professors in Europe hardly teach. European universities are, for the most part, a mess."

"I notice that most of the others on this identity project are from foreign universities. How did McInnis choose them?"

"He traveled a great deal and lectured all over the world, so he met them in the course of his visits to foreign universities. And he read a great deal, and when he found someone who had written a book that he found interesting, he'd get in touch with them and one thing led to another. Then when he got an advance from a publisher to edit a book on identity, he thought he'd try an experiment and arranged for us all to come on the cruise. Poor man . . . I never knew he had heart trouble. He always seemed so vigorous and full of life. And now . . . now, the poor man . . ."

Anastasia suddenly started crying.

"I'm sorry," she said, "but I can't help it. When I think of Marshall, I just . . . I get so upset. I had what you would call a 'love-hate' relationship with him. I think I'd best return to my cabin and rest for a while. It has been a terribly difficult day for me. Thanks, so much, for being such a good listener."

She shook hands with Solomon. He noticed she had a very firm grip.

"Yes, I understand," said Hunter. "I hope you'll feel better. Thanks for an extremely stimulating conversation."

Anastasia walked down some stairs, opened a door that led inside the ship, and disappeared. Hunter decided to go to the Atrium and get a drink.

Contemporary criticism has forced students and teachers to see that there are no innocent texts, that all artifacts of the established culture and society are laden with meaning, values, biases, and messages. There is no pure entertainment that does not contain representations—often extremely prejudicial—of class, gender, race, sexuality, and myriad social categories and groupings. Cultural texts are saturated with social meanings, they generate political effects, reproducing or opposing governing social institutions and relations of domination or subordination. Culture can embody specific political discourses—liberal, conservative, oppositional, or mixed—advancing competing political positions on issues such as the family and sexuality, masculinity or femininity, or violence and war. . . .

Culture in today's societies thus constitutes a set of discourses, stories, images, spectacles, and varying cultural forms and practices that generate meaning, identities, and political effects. Culture includes artifacts such as newspapers, television programs, movies, and popular music, but also practices like shopping, watching sports events, going to a club, or hanging out in the local coffee shop. Culture is ordinary, a part of everyday life, yet special cultural artifacts are extraordinary, helping people to see and understand things they've never quite perceived, like certain novels or films that change your view of the world. (6)

Douglas M. Kellner and Meenakshi Gigi Durham, "Adventures in Media and Cultural Studies: Introducing KeyWorks"

chapter **five**

Exploring the
Royal Duchess

"These modern cruise ships are enormous. The *Royal Duchess* is some-thing like eight hundred feet long and twelve stories high," thought Hunter. "It's like taking an eighty-story building and tipping it on its side. So there's a lot to see on this ship. And you never know what you'll find in the course of wandering around."

He decided to explore the ship. He walked to the forward part of the ship where large doors led to the casino. It was around 8:30 p.m., and his tablemates were still at the show, and passengers in the second sitting were still eating. To get to the casino you walked through a lounge area. A pianist and a woman singer were entertaining people, a few of whom were dancing. They were singing pop ballads. The casino was in a huge room that was bordered by rows of slot machines. For some reason, there weren't too many people gambling. Most of the people in the casino were watching the small group of dedicated gamblers who were playing blackjack or who were at the roulette table. The room was brightly lit and had a surrealistic quality to it.

Hunter walked around a bit and then left the casino area, walked down a flight of stairs, and found himself on the Lido Deck. There were several pools on this deck, including one that enabled people to swim to a bar and get their drinks while still in the water. The back part of the deck was devoted to a dining area called Café del Sol. It was where the buffets were served. There were two buffet lines, one on each side of the ship. Some people were eating there . . . from plates filled high with food.

He looked at the map of the liner that he was carrying. The next few decks seemed to have little of interest—just long hallways with cabins on either side—so he walked down until he reached deck seven, the Promenade Deck. The Palm Court dining room was at one end of the ship. The doors were closed because people were dining. Some passengers were standing on either side of the entrance to the Palm Court, looking at menus for the next day, which were posted there. There was also a line of couples who were waiting to have formal portraits of themselves taken. The men were in tuxedos and the women in evening gowns.

He turned to walk toward the forward part of the *Royal Duchess* and came upon the photo display area, where photos of the passengers were displayed. There were 1,600 passengers on the ship; half of their photos were on the side of the ship he was on, and the other half were on the other side of the ship. He decided to see if he could find Marshall McInnis's photo and photos of the other people at his table.

"I wonder what McInnis looked like alive," he thought. He was surprised to find that there were a goodly number of passengers in their thirties and forties, and plenty of children, too. He looked carefully at all the photographs but couldn't find McInnis or his colleagues, so he walked over to the other side of the ship to see if he could find them there. After a short while, he spotted McInnis, and then there were photos of all the others he had met at his table in the dining room. Hunter studied the photograph of McInnis carefully, looking for something that might be of interest. "I'm being a semiotician now, aren't I?" he thought.

After looking at the photographs, he started walking forward on the ship. In one lounge, a pianist was playing, and in another, a three-piece band was playing and some people were dancing. When he got to the Atrium, he walked down a couple of flights of stairs until he got to the Plaza. A pianist was playing show tunes. On one side of the Atrium, there was a long desk; it was the purser's office. On the other side was La Patisserie, a bar and coffee shop. In the middle of the Atrium, in the Plaza, there were tables where people were sitting, drinking.

"Funny," thought Hunter. "There are 1,600 passengers on this ship, but you don't see mobs of people anyplace. That may be because half of them are still eating and because a large number of the other passengers are at the show or watching movies in the Princess Theater." He walked up a couple of flights of stairs to deck eight, the Dolphin Deck, and after wandering around a bit, came to a large dancing hall, the Stage Door. People were sitting on either side of a sunken dancing area, drinking. A band was playing and some passengers were dancing. He continued walking forward and came to a small area, where there was a library, and, at the most forward part of the ship, the balcony of the International Show Lounge. He could hear someone playing a harmonica. "Just as well I skipped the show," he thought. "Harmonica players aren't my cup of tea." He consulted the map again. On deck three, five decks below, was the medical facility, and one deck below that, twelve decks below the casino, was the gym and spa area.

He was particularly fascinated by the faces of the passengers he encountered as he wandered around the ship. "Too bad Anastasia isn't here to analyze some of these people," he thought. "You can learn a lot from people's faces if you know what to look for. The problem is that some people don't have the faces they should have. Eco was right about lying with signs. They've learned how to disguise themselves, so there isn't a match between their faces and their characters. A lot of con artists have that clean-cut look that we tend to equate, in the popular mind, with honesty and upright behavior. That's how they get away with their crimes. And some people who don't have that look, whose eyes may be a touch too close together, who don't look at you straight in the eyes when they talk to you, are, it turns out, honest. So there is mystery to human identity and personality that poses important problems for semioticians like Anastasia. And policemen like me."

He noticed a man with a dark complexion and a thick mustache walking ahead of him, slowly.

"That's funny. I thought I noticed him a couple of other places I've been," he thought. "If I were more paranoid I'd think he was tailing me. But it's probably just a matter of coincidence.

"I think I'll call it a day as far as my explorations of the *Royal Duchess* are concerned," thought Hunter. "I've already walked off that dessert I had and the main course, at the very least. If you don't take elevators and walk up and down the long corridors, you get a lot of exercise. I've got a pretty good idea of what this liner is like. It's a little world to itself, but one dedicated, so it seems, mostly to eating, drinking, dancing, gambling, and having fun. A temporary escape from the real world, no doubt. It's like being back in the Garden of Eden—every need is taken care of. There's all the food you might want, there's entertainment . . . there's no end of things to do. You only have to pay for drinks. But no money passes hands, so you never get the sense that you're actually spending money. Then, when the cruise ends and you get the bill for your drinks and anything else you've spent money on, you're abruptly brought back into the real world. . . . Now that I think about it, I think I ought to get back to reality myself now and do a bit of speculating about where we are with this complicated investigation."

Hunter noticed that a large number of people suddenly had appeared in the hallways and were wandering about; apparently the show in the International Lounge had let out and the passengers who had been to the show were looking for more action. Groups of two and four people were chatting with one another. There were some people in wheelchairs who were being pushed along the corridor. A few children were wandering about.

Hunter glanced at his watch. It was 9:30 p.m. already. "I've been on the *Royal Duchess* more than five hours," he thought. "I've been very busy so far, but what have I learned? Am I making any progress with this investigation? You never know about these things. Sometimes you've picked up something very important, but you don't realize it at the time."

He decided to get a drink in the Plaza and listen to the pianist, when who should he see wandering around but Talcott Weems.

Weems saw him and came rushing over.

"How was the show?" asked Hunter.

"I loved it," said Weems. "They had this fantastic harmonica player. He was unbelievable. Just the kind of thing a person like me, with lowbrow taste, loves. And tomorrow, there's going to be a big show, with lots of singers and dancers. You've got to see it. We'll both go together."

Hunter nodded.

"I just had a long conversation with Anastasia," Hunter said. "At the end, when we got around to talking about Marshall McInnis, she started crying. She said they had a love-hate relationship. I found that quite interesting."

"Love and hate, eh? They often go together, don't they?" said Weems.

"Can I treat you to a drink, Talcott?" Hunter asked.

"Sounds great. I've got plenty to tell you about what I've been doing with myself, stuff that you'll find very interesting," he answered. "These professors. They really are something!"

Although the tourist need not be consciously aware of this, the thing he goes to see is society and its works. The societal aspect of tourist attractions is hidden behind their fame, but this fame cannot change their origin in social structure. Given the present sociohistorical epoch, it is not a surprise to find that tourists believe sightseeing is a leisure activity, and fun, even when it requires more effort and organization than many jobs. In a marked contrast to the grudging acquiescence that may characterize the relation of the individual to his industrial work, individuals happily embrace the attitudes and norms that lead them into a relationship with society through the sightseeing act. In being presented as a valued object through a so-called "leisure" activity that is thought to be "fun," society is renewed in the heart of the individual through warm, open, unquestioned relations, characterized by a near absence of alienation when compared with other contemporary relationships. (55)

Cruise lines are selling you a dream. . . . The power of your dream, your imagination, creates a challenge that the cruise industry is trying to meet. . . .

TV commercials and glossy color brochures about cruises all promise the same thing—an unexcelled excursion into the glamorous life, with romantic evenings, a perfect tan, six or eight gourmet meals a day, and intermittent forays into picturesque and exotic ports of call where the sun always shines, the shopping is splendid and the natives are friendly and photogenic.

Oddly enough, more often than not, it works out that way. (10, 11)

Dean MacCannell, *The Tourist: A New Theory of the Leisure Class*

Shirley Slater and Harry Basch, *Fielding's Alaska Cruises*

chapter **six**

ANTONIA SAID THAT ANASTASIA'S WORK WAS SECOND RATE

TALCOTT WEEMS REPORTS ON HIS INVESTIGATION

Talcott Weems Reports

Talcott Weems took a sip of his margarita.

"I usually just drink beer," he said, "but now that I'm on a cruise I might as well live it up!"

"Especially since the captain is paying," replied Hunter.

"I did a bit of investigative work on my own," said Weems. "After you left to go to that Palm Court dining hall, I decided to take a look at the people at your table in the flesh, so a few minutes after you left, I went in, showed my ticket to a waiter, and was being led to the table. But then, once I was able to see you and see what your tablemates looked like, I told the waiter I wasn't feeling well and wanted to go back to my room. So I went to that Café del Sol buffet and had a bite to eat. Buffets are a menace. I ate too much, I must admit. Then I wandered around the ship a bit and went to see the show. I made sure that I sat near your tablemates. They got there about fifteen or twenty minutes before the harmonica player went on. It turns out that for a half an hour before the show, the band plays music and a couple of really old geezers took the opportunity to dance on the stage. It was a kick.

"There were five of them at the show. They couldn't find a row with five empty seats, so three of them sat in one row and two of them in the row behind them. I managed to sit in the row behind the two people in the back row, the pretty Chinese woman and a guy in his midforties.

49

There seemed to be something going on between them. She was giving him 'the look' and fondling the hair on the back of his head. She was giggling at everything he said and saying things like 'Jean-Marie, you're so amusing' and 'Jean-Marie, you're such a naughty fellow.' And he would say things like 'Symphonie, you're simply divine.' When he turned to talk with her, I could see that he had that stupid look on his face that people have when they've been smitten. I take it he just met her on the trip. There was an older gentleman, a woman with short blonde hair—dyed, no doubt—and a redheaded woman in the row in front of them. And they all carried on a very interesting conversation with one another."

"So what did you learn?" asked Hunter.

"Well, at first they were all talking about you. They were trying to figure out what you did and what you were like. One of them, the redhead, said you were dressed too well to be a simple civil servant. 'Did you notice his suit and those fancy shoes?' she said. 'He's something of a dandy, though a little old to dress in such a preppy manner.' Someone wondered whether you'd gone to prep school on the East Coast. Another said that if you did work for the government, you probably were pretty high up in some important department. They were trying to explain why you weren't taking the cruise with your wife. 'Could he be a closet gay?' the old man wondered. But they said you didn't have any gay mannerisms and, besides, had a wedding ring. 'That means nothing!' said the old man, but they wouldn't buy his argument. They seemed to agree that there was something mysterious about you and that they would try to find out more about you the next evening at dinner."

"So—I'm going to get the once-over by these scholars. That should be most amusing," said Hunter.

"Then the conversation moved on to Anastasia. The redheaded woman didn't think very much of Anastasia's intellectual abilities—"

"Her name is Antonia," interrupted Hunter. "She's English."

"Yeah, I thought she had an English accent," replied Weems. "In any case, Antonia said she thought that Anastasia really shouldn't be one of the contributors to the book because her work was second-rate. 'Marshall only invited her to be one of the panel of writers,' she said, 'because he hoped he'd find a way to jump into bed with her. I guess that long blonde hair, those pointy breasts, and those bedroom green eyes snared him, the way they've snared any number of others. She's got ahead in the academic world not by having a first-class mind but by having round heels and her ability to find ways to make the two-backed beast so quickly.'"

"Did she sound jealous, or bitter? Or both?" asked Hunter.

"Hard to say," said Weems. "But I heard the Chinese woman whisper to Jean-Marie that she was angry because this McInnis fellow had dropped her to have an affair with Katarina and then dropped Katarina to chase after Anastasia. I take it McInnis had given a lecture in Italy and met Anastasia and decided he wanted to add her name to his list of conquests. The Chinese woman told Jean-Marie that there was talk that Anastasia was a closet lesbian, or maybe a bisexual. So he didn't realize what a big mistake he was making."

"No fool like a middle-aged fool," said Hunter.

"What I don't get," said Weems, "is why all these women who had been dumped by McInnis would agree to take a cruise with him and work on a book? It doesn't make sense."

"Maybe they hoped to win him back? You never know," replied Hunter. "Or they thought they'd have a good time and get a good publication out of the trip. It isn't easy to figure out why people do things, especially why they kill one another. You know that as well as I do!"

"The old guy two rows in front of me, what's his name?" asked Weems.

"Sigfried Duerfklein," said Hunter. "He's a shrink."

"So this Sigfried fellow," said Weems, "then ventures an opinion that Anastasia probably is a nymphomaniac and should be pitied rather than scorned. He said she has all the classical hallmarks of nymphos, including the ability to attract satyromaniacs, their polar opposites, like McInnis, and this was probably connected with her infancy and her relations with her mother.

"'I don't agree,' said the woman with the dark brown hair. 'The trouble with you, Sigfried, is that you're a prisoner of your Freudian perspectives on everything. And everything in your way of seeing things is connected to infant sexuality, the Oedipus complex, and unconscious drives that ultimately control everyone. It's all too simplistic.'"

"Her name is Katarina," said Hunter.

"'No,' said Katarina, 'I don't think Marshall was a sex maniac. I think he was like a fly that just got caught in a web spun by Anastasia. She's known by everyone in the field for having round heels, and well known in other ways—if you get what I mean—by a rather large number of scholars. She's actually a manipulative careerist who uses that long blonde hair and her sexy figure to get ahead. She's a determined and very calculating woman, which she disguises very well. Russian women, though they're often very beautiful when they're young, usually end up dumpy and sexless when they hit forty or forty-five. So she's only got five or ten years to go before everything falls apart for her. I rather pity her.'

"'We were told that Marshall died of a heart attack,' said Symphonie. 'But I wonder whether it could have been something else—like suicide. Marshall was very moody and had a dark side to him that he managed to keep hidden from others. When I was married to him, I discovered that he wasn't the happy-go-lucky, good-natured, witty person I thought he was. Maybe he killed himself and they're keeping that from us.'

"'If he did kill himself,' said Antonia, 'it was because he finally realized that he wasn't an important thinker. He was, I'd say, a rather clever but superficial thinker, with a marvelous gift for self-promotion. If you think about it, did he have any original ideas? All of his books are basically rewrites and amplifications of the work of others. He was a trickster, an amusing fellow who had a flair for catchy phrases but left nothing behind that will last.'

"'When you put it that way,' said Jean-Marie, 'it would seem that Marshall and Anastasia were well suited for one another. Could he have recognized, somehow, that it was her mediocrity that attracted him to her rather than her glamour?'

"'Don't be silly, Jean-Marie,' said Katarina. 'Men are, for the most part, stupid animals, ready to screw up their lives and toss aside their wives of twenty or thirty years for some dim-witted glamour girl who will become one of those trophy wives we read about. But there's more to a relationship than sex, and I always sense that these older men with their trophy wives have a kind of sadness about them, as if they somehow realize what they've done and what they've become. I think they're pathetic. They're actually victims and tend to be depressed, even though they may not recognize that such is the case.'

"'In this, I agree with you,' said Duerfklein. 'Marriages of May and December generally are a disaster. It often turns out, ironically, that it is the older husband who is the trophy for the younger woman. He's the trophy, and the prize that comes with it is his bank account. It's a very sad matter.'

"'I've read that there is a good deal of crime on these liners,' added Jean-Marie. 'There are often articles about rapes and robbery on cruises in the newspaper. Do you think one of the crew members could have murdered Marshall?'

"'Murdered him?' said Antonia. 'It would have served him right, but I doubt that anyone in the crew would have gone that far. He told me he was going to get on the ship early, around 1:00 p.m. I believe. And he must have died sometime in the next few hours, since the ship sailed at 5:00 p.m. That wouldn't leave him much time to get into trouble, let alone get murdered. But if anyone could have managed to do so, it would be Marshall. Still, I can't imagine that he was murdered.'

"'There could be someone on the ship whom we don't know about, who harbored a hatred for him. It's always possible,' said Symphonie. 'People like Marshall often make a lot of enemies.'

"'This conversation is getting pretty crazy,' said Katarina. 'Let's talk about something else.'

"She turned to Antonia.

"'How is your chapter coming?' Katarina asked.

"Just then, the band started playing loudly, and a slender man with a thin mustache came running up on the stage.

"'Hello, everyone,' he said. 'My name is Tommy Pynchon, and I'm the cruise director. My job is to make sure everyone has a wonderful time on this cruise. Are you having fun so far?'

"Many people in the audience clapped.

"'Are you getting enough to eat?'

"People in the audience shouted, 'Yes, yes.'

"'Remember,' Tommy said. 'You come on as passengers and you'll leave as cargo! But think of how great it was getting there. Well, we've got a truly fabulous show for you tonight and, as a matter of fact, every night here at the Show Lounge. There'll be a huge show tomorrow, called "C'est Magnifique," that will have our singers and dancers and the *Royal Duchess* band, and the night after, we've got a marvelous singer to entertain you. Ladies and gentlemen—she really is sensational, and I'm sure you'll all love her. And that's the way it's going to be every night on the *Royal Duchess*. We want you to have a really great time on this cruise. Remember, of course, we have a casino and dancing until all hours of the night in a number of places. And remember, you can purchase superb works of art at our fabulous art auction in the Bengal Lounge. But enough of that. If I told you about all the incredible things you can do on this cruise, it would take an hour. So let's get the show on the road with a truly remarkable artist, an incredible virtuoso on his instrument, the mouth organ. He is a world-famous musician, and you'll know why when you hear him!'"

"So you saw a harmonica player," said Hunter.

"Yes. And he was very good, too. Of course, that killed the chit-chat by the professors, so I didn't learn anything else. They seemed to be enjoying the harmonica player, too. After the show, I went looking for you to tell you what I learned."

"Good work, Talcott," said Hunter. "With the information you gave me, I can have a little fun with our professors over the course of the cruise. And maybe learn something of interest, too."

They were interrupted by the chief of security, who came rushing toward them. He was carrying a large manila envelope.

"Mr. Hunter. At last I've found you," he said. "I have something interesting for you." He lowered his voice. "I have a report that was sent to you by your office. I think it also has something from Interpol. We just printed out the e-mail message."

He handed Hunter the envelope.

Weems was looking around at a crowd of people that had suddenly materialized on the deck above them and noticed Anastasia there, too.

"There's Anastasia," Weems said. "Looks like she decided to get a drink." He caught her eye and beckoned to her. He pointed to the table, indicating she should come and join them.

Anastasia was at the top of the stairwell and about to descend when a woman who was behind her suddenly tripped and fell against Anastasia. The woman screamed. A man who was walking behind the woman grabbed her, so she didn't fall, but Anastasia found herself off balance and about to lurch down the stairs.

"My God," said Weems. "She's going to fall down the stairs. She'll break her neck!"

Anastasia fell forward, but she somehow was able to place her right foot on one of the stairs and do a pirouette that enabled her to fall against a railing. She grabbed on to the railing and held on for a few seconds. She was breathing very hard and trembling when Hunter and the security director reached her.

"You almost had a nasty fall," said Hunter. "If you hadn't found a way to flip your leg over, you might have been seriously injured, or even killed."

"Yes, I know," said Anastasia. "Fortunately, I had those years of ballet training and my legs are very strong. But I'm OK now. It was just an accident."

"Yes, just an accident," said the security director, nervously. "Just an accident."

"Come, join us for a drink," said Hunter. "You need to relax, and you could use some company."

"Yes, you're right," said Anastasia. "I could use a Stoli."

"Just an accident?" wondered Hunter. "But what if it wasn't just an accident?"

The individual has become a mere cog in an enormous organization of things and powers which tear from his hands all progress, spirituality, and value in order to transform them from their subjective form into the form of a purely objective life. It needs merely to be pointed out that the metropolis is the genuine arena of this culture which outgrows all personal life. Here in buildings and educational institutions, in the wonders and comforts of space-conquering technology, in the formations of community life, and in the visible institutions of the state, is offered such an overwhelming fullness of crystallized and impersonalized spirit that the personality, so to speak, cannot maintain itself under its impact. On the one hand, life is made infinitely easy for the personality in that stimulations, interests, uses of time and consciousness are offered to it from all sides. They carry the person as if in a stream, and one needs hardly to swim for oneself. On the other hand, however, life is composed more and more of these impersonal contents and offerings which tend to displace the genuine personal colorations and incomparabilities. This results in the individual's summoning the utmost in uniqueness and particularization, in order to preserve his most personal core. He has to exaggerate this personal element in order to remain audible even to himself. (184)

Georg Simmel, *The Metropolis and Mental Life* (quoted in *Simmel on Culture*, edited by David Frisby and Mike Featherstone)

chapter seven

"THIS CASE IS A TANGLED KNOT" SAID HUNTER

Interpol
Report
TOP
SECRET

The Interpol Report

After their drink with Anastasia, Hunter and Weems returned to their cabin. Weems opened the manila envelope with the report.

"Here's the summary of the report from the autopsy," said Weems. He started reading it:

Autopsy number: 113181-36A-2004
Sharp force injury: penetrating stab wound to left back with
     hemothorax, perforation of left lung.
Blood ethanol: *0.11*

Clinicopathological correlation: Cause of death is due to a sharp force injury to the back. The lack of decomposition on external examination is consistent with a postmortem of between one and three hours. The external genitalia are unremarkable and show no evidence of injury or trauma. The upper and lower extremities show no deformities. There is a dried whitish substance on the penile shaft and upper right anterior thigh which appears to be semen. Stab wound to left side of back. The stab wound is located 23 inches from the crown of the head and 41 inches from the sole, and 6 inches from the midline. The wound is vertically orientated and after approximation of the edges it measures 7/8 inches in length. The

57

wound path is through the skin, subcutaneous tissue, and through the left 7th rib. The rib is totally incised. This is a fatal wound associated with perforation of the left lung and hemothorax. The wound is consistent with a knife wound, the abraded edge inferiorly suggestive of penetration of a blade with a serrated edge.

"That autopsy report is interesting," said Hunter. "It seems that McInnis had sex shortly before he was murdered. That may be important."

Weems scanned the report.

"There was nothing to speak of in his computer, though. Just a bunch of letters and some articles about media and stuff like that."

"Not much to go on so far," said Hunter.

"But Interpol has come through with stuff about the professors at our table."

"Anything interesting?" asked Hunter.

"Take a look for yourself," said Weems. He passed the papers to Hunter.

"This McInnis was a very busy and complicated person," said Hunter. "He was married three times. First, to someone named Joyce Jameson, for quite a while. Then to a woman named Svetlana Chesnok for five years, and then to Symphonie for a few months. He really got around. Was a visiting professor all over. It seems he was hardly in Los Angeles for more than a semester every year. He taught in London, in Budapest, in Vienna, in Milan, in Moscow, in Beijing."

He stopped for a moment.

"Symphonie's from Beijing, isn't she?"

"Yeah," said Weems.

"That's interesting," replied Hunter. "I think I'll look at what Interpol has to say about Symphonie."

Hunter shuffled through some pages until he came to the Interpol material on Symphonie.

"She comes from a well-to-do and very distinguished family," said Hunter. "Her father was a physician, and her mother was a judge. She has a brother, Xian, who's the president of a bank in Hong Kong, and a twin sister, Mei Ling, who, it turns out, was a criminal involved in all kinds of shady deals and maybe even some murders. She had a record a yard long. It seems that she died suddenly, last year, from a heart attack. Isn't it ironic the way you have a mother for a judge and a daughter who becomes a criminal? Symphonie's real name, that is, her Chinese name, is Siu Lau."

"Siu Lau and Symphonie. Not very close, but they both start with an *s*," said Weems.

"Chinese men and women often take Western names to make it easy for people who don't speak Chinese to remember their names," said Hunter. "She's very brilliant, according to this report. She won a lot of scholarships, was first in her class everywhere, and graduated with highest honors from Beijing University. Now she's a professor at the Beijing Broadcast Institute. Maybe Beijing's where the connection with McInnis comes in? He spent a semester in Beijing. He might have met her there."

"And now she's involved with that Benetton guy. These professors. They lead complicated lives, I can see that," said Weems. "Benetton, from what I could see, was really smitten. I can understand why. Symphonie's as beautiful as she is smart—what a fantastic combination. She almost sounds too good to be true!"

"Some people have all the luck, Talcott," said Hunter. "Since you mentioned Benetton, I think I'll see what Interpol has to say about him."

He shuffled the pages until he came to Benetton.

"He's another smart guy. Now he's at this famous government center the French have for their most brilliant social scientists. But get this, Talcott—he's married. To a psychologist, Justine Kristeva. Graduated from the University of Paris and then went to one of their 'Grandes Ecoles' and taught at the University of Paris."

"These professors may be smart but they aren't very moral, as far as I can tell," said Weems.

"They're no different from anyone else," said Hunter. "We're all human beings, and we all can be tempted. Sometimes temptation is pretty hard to resist. I guess Benetton would say that being faithful to your wife is modernist and thus passé in a postmodern world. I guess affairs are the gold standard now."

He read through the rest of the material from Interpol.

"Antonia Fathom, the redhead. She's a real star, it seems. Graduated with a first at Oxford. That takes some doing."

"What's a first?" asked Weems.

"In English universities, they have this system where really remarkable students are recognized and graduate with firsts, others graduate with seconds, and so on. If you graduate with a first in Britain, it means you're a real superstar. She wrote a book, *The Rhetoric of Identity*, that's one of the bibles of the feminists, it says here."

"Anything interesting on that tall blonde?" asked Weems.

Hunter looked through the report.

"Let's see. Anastasia Lotman. Nothing that strikes my attention. She was married to an Italian count; now she teaches semiotics in Bologna. Nothing about another marriage in here. She told me she was married to someone from Tartu, if I remember correctly. That's one of the centers of her discipline. There's a touch of irony here, Talcott. You found out from Benetton, if I recall correctly, that McInnis dumped Antonia to settle in with Katarina and then abandoned her to chase after Anastasia, not realizing that she's probably a lesbian. We don't know whether Symphonie is right about that. After all, Anastasia was married twice and according to others she's a nymphomaniac with very round heels."

"Lesbians can have round heels, too," added Weems. "Just like any other woman."

"That's a good point, Talcott," said Hunter. "This whole story is full of contradictions and rather incestuous and complicated relationships. McInnis seems to have slept with or was sleeping with or trying to sleep with every woman on the team."

"I guess he had a lot of energy," said Weems.

"This case is really a tangled knot, with strings leading all over the damned place and intertwined with one another everywhere," said Hunter. "I don't know how I'll ever untangle it. I have this sense that there's something that explains it all that I've already come across, something that I know about, but I can't put my finger on it. It's like having a word on the tip of your tongue. Duerfklein would say it's in my preconscious, waiting for me to uncover it."

H. Leslie Steeves and
Marilyn Crafton Smith,
"Class and Gender in
Prime-Time Television
Entertainment:
Observations from a
Socialist Feminist
Perspective"

Charles Winick,
Desexualization in
American Life

In contrast to liberal feminists, socialist feminists, as Marxists, assume that the class system under capitalism is fundamentally responsible for women's oppression. At the same time they agree with radical feminists that "patriarchy" (gender oppression) is fundamental in its own right and certainly existed long before capitalism. Thus, most socialist feminists argue that patriarchy and capitalism must be simultaneously addressed, largely via the eradication of divided labor by both gender and class. Also, in contrast to liberal feminists' focus on how media affects individual attitudes and behaviors, socialist feminists emphasize the centrality of media (and other communication processes, such as language, education and art) in actually constructing ideology, including the ideology of women's secondary status. (43–44)

Archaeologists of the future may regard a radical dislocation of sexual identity as the single most important event of our time. Ethology, the science concerned with animal behavior and interaction, has repeatedly hinted in recent years that radical changes in sex roles may lead to extermination of whole species. This does not mean that we, the New People, will fail to survive or that we are unable to create a viable substitute for rejected lifestyles. It does suggest that the new tone of life, a bitter, metallic existence, may simply not be worth the price of enduring it. . . . The [atom] bomb is the model of the new technology that is profoundly affecting every aspect of social and sex roles. The decline of romantic love reflects and reinforces other changes that are modifying expressions of the most basic difference in any society—the difference between its men and women. (xi)

chapter eight

Antonia Fathom

It was 7:30 a.m. on the second day of the cruise. The *Royal Duchess* was to be at sea all day, heading for Victoria, its first port. Hunter decided to get a bit of fresh air before having breakfast. Weems was snoring away when Hunter got dressed. The captain had sent them two suitcases full of clothes, to make it seem that they were regular passengers. Hunter decided to go up to the Sun Deck and stroll around for a bit. To get there, he had to go through the Lido buffet area. There were already a number of people who were having breakfast at the buffet. Hunter walked through the buffet area, out onto the deck, and then up a flight of stairs to the Sun Deck. He started walking on the deck and, to his surprise, came across Antonia Fathom, who was wearing a stylish workout suit.

"Hello, Antonia," he said. "I see you're dedicated to the good life. Getting some exercise, so you can work off last night's dinner. Mind if I walk around with you?"

"My pleasure," she said. "I'm trying to prepare for tonight's dinner. If I do enough turns around the deck, I believe that I can eat whatever I want and not gain any weight."

"As long as you go easy on the desserts," cautioned Hunter. "How was the show last night?" he asked.

"Have you ever had to sit through an hour of someone playing the harmonica?" she asked. "Ten minutes would have been fine, but an hour was an eternity. I kept thinking he'd be stopping and they'd bring someone else on, but he kept playing and playing. From a sociological perspective, it was an interesting experience. That means it was actually a crushing bore. But we were all together, having a bit of fun, and it took our minds off of Marshall's death for a while."

"That has some value," said Hunter.

"And how was your walk with Anastasia?"

"Very interesting," said Hunter. "She came close to having a nasty fall last night. She almost fell down the stairs leading to the Plaza Lounge."

"Poor thing. I hope she wasn't too traumatized," said Antonia.

"No, she's fine," replied Hunter. "She had a drink with us and seemed to be OK when she left us to go to bed."

"When you were walking with her, did she give you her semiotics of blondeness routine? She's brilliant, you know, and has made some truly important contributions to semiotics. We tend to think that beautiful women are shallow and dumb, or maybe we hope they are. It doesn't seem fair that some women should be both beautiful and very clever while others are plain and not very smart at all. Anastasia's very smart and knows it, too. But she tends to use her material a bit too long."

"You've heard it?" asked Hunter.

"At every conference she's ever been at. All that sign stuff is interesting, but semiotics, despite its arcane jargon, is totally superficial. Semioticians think that semiotics is the key to everything. They see every academic discipline as being, in essence, a subcategory of semiotics, and they reduce human beings to sign-generating and sign-interpreting animals, and by doing so, they neglect the human psyche and, of particular interest to me, the power of language. Anastasia and her fellow semioticians do have some fascinating things to say, but in the final analysis, their conclusions, to my mind, miss the point. Everything may be a sign, but so what? Human beings are more than sign-sending and sign-receiving animals.

"When semioticians analyze literary texts, for example, they neglect aesthetic matters in their search for signs and the codes that tie signs together. They reduce novels, films, plays, television shows, commercials—whatever you want to talk about—to little more than collections of signs that are related to one another in curious ways. Generally, to binary oppositions. It's analogous to judging dinner on the *Royal Duchess* by the quality of the ingredients and saying nothing about how they are cooked. And that's typical of semioticians. They make clever, often ingenious, analyses, but you never know whether what they are saying is correct or sheer fantasy. Semiotics has all kinds of abstruse theories but no predictive power. It isn't empirical. In the final analysis, semioticians reduce everything to human consciousness and don't pay enough attention to the outside world and the role of social and political forces in shaping our language and thought. That's why a number of scholars think semioticians are, to a considerable degree, academic charlatans.

"I speak, of course, as a linguist and a rhetorician. We're interested in the power of language. This interest and our discipline goes back as far as Aristotle, who dealt with language and its role in human affairs. Linguistics, unlike semiotics, is an empirical science, with theories and strong predictive powers."

"I'm not an academic," said Hunter, "so I hope you'll excuse me. But how does rhetoric fit in with this business of identity that you and your colleagues are working on? It's not clear to me."

"Think," she said, "about babies. How do they learn about the world? From the languages of their mothers and fathers. There are two aspects to this. First, there is the language spoken—French, German, Italian, English, Chinese, whatever. Second, there is the way a baby's parents and those around the baby speak. An English sociolinguist named Basil Bernstein studied the way working-class and upper-class parents spoke to their children and used language in general and discovered that there were considerable differences between the two."

"Is that so?" replied Hunter.

"Yes. He called the language used by working-class people the 'restricted' code, and it was characterized by being grammatically simple; using short, repetitive sentences; using few adjective and adverbs;

having few qualifications; and being emotional. On the other hand, the middle and upper classes used the 'elaborated' code. It was grammatically complex, used complicated sentence structures, included the careful use of adjectives and adverbs, and was logical. It was a good preparation for higher education."

"Why is this important?" asked Hunter.

"These codes then become a matrix through which a child gains understanding of the world. So babies raised in working-class families tend to be present-minded and not concerned about the consequences of actions and the future. Working-class children see the world differently from children in middle- and upper-class families. And what's most important, from my perspective, as a feminist, is that working-class children also learn how to relate to women differently from children of middle- and upper-class families. You don't find too many men who are sympathetic to the feminist cause in the trades and doing what you Yanks call 'blue-collar' work!"

"So it's language that's basic for you?" asked Hunter.

"Language as it shapes culture and, ultimately, identity. I believe we're all hardwired for language. It's a controversial matter, but there's good evidence to suggest that the ability to understand language is something we're born with. My colleagues are dealing with identity, but identity, for them, is always secondary, always part of something else—class, race, whatever. But gender is something you're born with. Let's face it— you're born either a male or a female. So gender is natural, and, to my mind, of immense significance."

"I can see that," replied Hunter.

"This is important," she continued. "Race may be socially constructed. Is a person whose mother is black and father white considered to be black or white? It all depends on where you live and how people think about things like this. But gender is a given. Except, of course, for transsexuals, who live as women in men's bodies or men in women's bodies or a small number who actually change their gender. There are surgeons in Tangiers who have expertise in that matter. But for most people, you are born a male or a female and stay as such. However, the way females are treated in society is connected to the culture in which they are raised. If you are unfortunate enough to be born a female in Afghanistan, you will wear a burka so nobody outside your house can ever see your face, while if you are born in the United States, depending on the fashion, you may wear low-rider jeans and wear jewels in your belly button. I understand Britney Spears is passé now, so maybe young girls will start covering themselves up again. In Brazil, at the beach, if you are a woman, you will have a bathing suit that is made of eight or ten inches of material total."

"Let me see if I understand you," said Hunter. "You're arguing that language shapes culture, and culture determines the way men relate to women."

"Yes, but also how women think of themselves and the way they relate to one another and to men. It takes two to tango," she replied. "But all of this connects, ultimately, with identity, for, as I see things, gender is all-important in people's identities. Your culture or subculture teaches you how to be a woman or a man and what kind of woman or man to become. The problem is that all societies are—and pardon me if I use a technical term—all societies are 'phallocentric.' That means that our cultures are all organized, at the unconscious level of course, around the male phallus. There were ancient cultures that worshipped the male phallus. They actually made statues of giant penises called lingams. Now, in contemporary societies, we construct gigantic skyscrapers—tall buildings that serve the same function of symbolizing the patriarchy, the domination of males over females.

"Men, of course, assume that the power relationships they find in society, in which they are dominant, are natural, and so they cannot recognize that women are generally subordinated. What we feminists argue is that the various institutions found in these patriarchal societies and the roles played by men in these societies are all shaped by male sexuality and the power of the male phallus. Men cannot recognize this and generally react with shock and often with ridicule when feminists make this argument.

"Feminists," she continued, "are also concerned with a phenomenon we call the 'male gaze,' in which men look at women as nothing but sexual objects. Women are generally portrayed in the mass media as sexual objects, and what really bothers feminists is that many women, taking their cues from the media, take pleasure in presenting themselves as sexual objects."

"But the people involved in all this don't recognize this. That's your point, isn't it?" asked Hunter.

"Yes, it all goes on at the unconscious level. Think, for example, of George Washington, the so-called father of your country. When you wanted to construct a monument to him, what did you do? You built the Washington Monument, a gigantic penis sticking up into the sky. A perfect symbol for a phallocentric culture. And now, in an age of terrorists, you're all scared—scared stiff, as you often put it, an interesting term from a linguistic point of view—that terrorists will try to blow up the Washington Monument, in essence symbolically castrating you."

Antonia looked into Hunter's eyes and smiled.

"I hope I'm not boring you. You know what professors are like. Just get them started and they'll run off at the mouth forever, explaining their pet theories. From my perspective, women lose any chance of obtaining secure identities by constantly assuming different roles—cheerleader, bride, secretary, and mother. They become caught up in momentary things and everyday pursuits and seldom, except for the very strong, have enough energy to become themselves. Their identities become diffused. They become so adept at hiding their real identities so well that eventually they either can't find them or forget about them. And they find it difficult to think about themselves because they are forced to use languages that, I would argue, are masculine in nature. Women are searching for a feminine rhetoric, you could say, so they can talk about themselves, and think about themselves, more intelligently and more realistically.

"There's something else to consider. When we are young, most of us have some notion of something big and important that we want to do with our lives. What happens, however, is that we get caught up with this and that distraction in our everyday lives. And before we know it, what we find is that our lives are consumed by the distractions and we forget about the great thing we hoped to do. This is especially a problem with women, who often find their lives preoccupied with raising their children."

Antonia stopped. "Does this make sense to you?"

"Yes, it does," replied Hunter. "I'm getting an excellent education on this cruise. I have to confess—I'd never thought much about identity. I don't imagine most people do. And now I find a group of scholars obsessed about the matter."

"That's right," she said. "Most people just live from day to day and never really think too much about how they arrive at themselves. We just get caught up in our activities and affairs, and before we know it, we're old and never really got to know ourselves. We dissipate ourselves and scatter our identities. Some people keep changing and modifying their identities, including their gender identities, and never attain a stable one. Their identity relates back to a rather primitive matter, which is where this conversation started—boy or girl. Did you know that pink used to be the color for boys and blue for girls? Isn't that interesting? In the final analysis, we pick up gender codes, from our language and culture, about how to act, what to do, what to be, and spend the rest of our lives following them. Identity is a fascinating problem when you start thinking about it, and feminist theory has a lot to say about it. There are a number of scholars, such as Elaine Showalter, bell hooks, and Helene Cixous, who have done important work on various aspects of feminist thought and made it a major consideration for scholars nowadays.

"There's a feminist scholar, Judith Butler, who takes issue with the idea of some feminist thinkers who, she argues, accept the traditional notions of gender and sex. Her ideas are quite similar, in interesting ways, to those of dear old Sigfried. She argues, and I'm simplifying things a bit, that gender is a kind of performance and that our genders can be considered impersonations, so to speak; they are not the expression of our real selves or essential 'inner' cores. Our gender identities are, in a way, parodies that are shaped, to a considerable extent, by the social and political situations in which we find ourselves. Her theory enables her to attack the notion of what might be called 'compulsory heterosexuality,' the idea that heterosexuality is and must be the only norm in societies. Butler's ideas play an important role in a field of study called 'queer theory.' It builds upon her argument that gender is socially constructed and is a performance. She attacks the traditional binary view of gender and sex that most people take for granted. It's all quite complicated . . . and goes back, ultimately, to Saussure's notions about the way language works."

"And what about you?" asked Hunter. "How did you become Antonia Fathom? How did you arrive at yourself? How did you become a feminist? And is there a real Antonia Fathom, or is what you seem to be merely a performance?"

"I can see that you're an excellent student, Solomon," she replied. "And you have good questions to ask your instructor. As you can tell, from my accent, I'm English and from the educated classes. I speak what you Americans call the Queen's English—what's called in England 'the received pronunciation.' My father was a Harley Street physician and my mother was a dentist. There are lots of women dentists in England, or used to be when I was growing up. Now, thankfully, many women are going into medicine. Having the advantages of being born into an educated and prosperous family, I received an excellent education, went up to Oxford, where I became interested in language, managed to marry a fellow student and get divorced a few years later, and after a short stay at a red-brick school, on the basis of some books I wrote, I was offered a position at Oxford."

"Yes," said Hunter. "That's your résumé. But what about the real you lurking behind that résumé? What kind of person are you? You seem to be kind and generous. I noticed that you said nice things about Anastasia. Other women, who had picked up the wrong codes, as you would put it . . . might be catty and very nasty about a woman like her. Beautiful women often inspire really nasty gossip."

"That's kind of you, Hunter," she said. "I can see you're really a gentleman. Let me be truthful now. Last night, at the show, we all talked about you. We all have our doubts about your being just a civil servant. You dress too well and you listen too well. No, we don't buy that description."

"But it's true," Hunter insisted.

"It may be true, but we doubt if you're telling us the whole truth. So we're all trying to figure out who you really are and what you really do. You realize, of course, that we're all extremely—maybe obsessively—curious about people: about their identities and about why they do what they do."

"So am I," replied Hunter. "Lots of people are interested in why people do the things they do. Understanding human motivation and being able to predict and figure out human behavior isn't restricted to professors, or anyone. It turns out I have many of your interests, but I don't approach the matter like you and your colleagues, on a scholarly and theoretical level."

"Ha!" said Antonia. "You've told me nothing, which means I won't have anything of consequence to report to my colleagues when we next get together. But we'll keep prying."

"Keep prying and, who knows, you might have a big surprise!" said Hunter.

"A bit of a wit, too," replied Antonia. "And so early in the morning."

"I'm getting hungry," said Hunter. "Would you care to join me for breakfast in the Palm Court?"

"No thanks," said Antonia. "I'm going to do a few more laps, have a bite in the Café de Sol, and get to work on my chapter. We've all committed to finishing our chapters by the time the ship returns to San Francisco. It will take a bit of doing."

Nigel Dennis,

Cards of Identity

Sigmund Freud, *Group Psychology and the Analysis of the Ego*

You must try and understand that the old days are over—the days when you could take your identity for granted. Nowadays, all the old means of self-recognition have been swept away, leaving even the best people in a state of personal dubiety. Even dis-possession, the surest means of bringing home the naked identity, has disappeared. Very wisely, gov-ernments all over the world have sought to stop this rot before the entire human population has been re-duced to anonymous grains. They give you cards, on which they inscribe in capital letters the name which your fading memory supplies before it is too late. It is their hope that by continually reading and re-reading your *name*, you will be able to keep hold of a past that no longer exists, and thus bring an il-lusion of self into the present. (94)

The contrast between Individual Psychology and Social or Group Psychology, which at first glance may seem to be full of significance, loses a great deal of its sharpness when it is examined more closely. It is true that Individual Psychology is con-cerned with the individual man and explores the paths by which he seeks to find satisfaction for his instincts; but only rarely and under certain excep-tional conditions is Individual Psychology in a posi-tion to disregard the relations of this individual to others. In the individual's mental life someone else is invariably involved as a model, as an object, as a helper, as an opponent, and so from the very first Individual Psychology is at the same time Social Psychology as well. (169–70) ✦

chapter nine

I SEE DARK CLOUDS, I SENSE DANGER ...

The Psychic

When Hunter entered the Palm Court that morning, there were a number of waiters standing at the entrance, ready to lead people to a table.

"I'd like a table near a window," said Hunter.

"Very fine, sir," said one of the waiters. "Please follow me."

The waiter led Hunter to the back of the dining hall, which was just half full. The waiter spied a table for six near a window and led Hunter to it. There was a rather stout gentleman with a long gray beard who looked as if he was in his late sixties sitting there, talking to a woman with curly gray hair on the other side of the table. He had large blue suspenders to keep his pants up. When they noticed that the waiter had brought Hunter over, they turned to him and smiled.

"Good morning," the man said. "My name is Bill Riley, and this lovely woman here, sitting across the table from me, is my wife, Mabel."

"Hi," said Mabel. "I guess you like tables near windows, like us."

"Yes," said Hunter. "I rather enjoy being able to look out at the ocean. My name is Solomon Hunter."

A waiter appeared with a menu and gave it to Hunter. An assistant waiter brought a glass of ice water. Hunter studied the menu. There were several rather exotic-sounding fruit dishes, as well as standards like French toast and steak and eggs with hash brown potatoes. A waiter who was circulating among the tables with a large tray with a plastic dome over it came over.

"Would you like a croissant or a sweet roll?" he asked.

Hunter took a croissant to munch on while he waited to give his order.

A waiter came over.

"Are you ready to order, sir?" he asked.

"I'd like a glass of orange juice, a plain yogurt, some steak and eggs, over light, with hash browned potatoes, and a cappuccino," he said.

"Very good, sir," said the waiter.

"I worked up a good appetite walking around the top deck," Hunter said to his new tablemates.

"Yes, walking in the sea air always makes you hungry," said Mabel. "I see you're having breakfast by yourself. Is your wife sleeping in?"

"My wife is in San Francisco," replied Hunter. "I'm here with a friend. We got a free cruise. The price was right, so we figured we'd give it a try. My cabinmate is eating in the cabin. He ordered room service, says he wants to see how the fancy people live. So I'm out on my own."

"Is this your first cruise?" asked Bill.

"Yes," replied Hunter.

"This is our fifteenth," said Bill. "Mabel and I like to cruise, and once I retired from Pacific Gas and Electric, where I was a foreman, we decided to live it up. And cruising is the best way we know how to do that."

"I love cruises," said Mabel. "You don't have to cook and clean up afterward, the food's wonderful, you unpack once, and you meet the most interesting people."

"That's true," said Hunter. "For the evening meals my friend and I were put at a table full of professors. They're all on the cruise together, working on a book on identity."

"Identity," said Bill. "What's there to say about that? You know what a person does and you have most of it right there. You said the folks at your table were professors. That's their identity as I see things. There may be other things, but it's your job that tells the world who you are. You are what you do."

"You know professors," said Hunter. "They find ways of making everything complicated. Whatever the case, they've agreed to spend every day writing for a period and then have fun the rest of the day. That doesn't sound too bad to me."

"Me neither," said Mabel.

"Since we're dealing with occupations, and you mentioned cooking and cleaning, were you, by chance, a housewife?" asked Hunter.

"No, not at all," she replied. "I'm a gifted psychic and have been one for many years."

"A psychic!" replied Hunter.

"Yes! You have to be born with the gift, but you also learn things over the years. You learn how to observe people, and you get some notions about them just from the way they walk and dress and what their voices sound like and the expressions on their faces. I learned I was a psychic about thirty years ago, just by accident. And since then, I've been using the gift the good Lord gave me!"

"She's helped countless numbers of people," said Bill. "She's done a lot of good, mostly for ordinary people, who can't afford those high-priced psychiatrists and psychologists. All they want to do, it seems, is give you pills or have you talk about your mother."

The waiter brought Bill an order of French toast and Mabel a toasted bagel and a poached egg.

"In a sense, then, you're in the identity business, too," said Hunter. "You help people discover things about themselves. Things that will help them."

"Yes," said Mabel. "I'm on vacation and have temporarily turned off my psychic powers, you could say, but suddenly, for some reason, I've got some very strong messages about you. I can't explain it. Just in the last couple of minutes."

She stared at Hunter.

The waiter brought Hunter his breakfast and Hunter started eating. Bill was eating his French toast and looked longingly at Hunter's steak and eggs.

"That sure looks good," said Bill. "I was going to order steak and eggs myself but thought it might be a bit too heavy."

"It really is delicious," Hunter said. "Would you like to try a bit of mine? I can cut off a bit of steak and give you some of my eggs. There's plenty."

"No, I'd better not," he replied. "But I'm kicking myself for not getting the steak and eggs, now that I see what yours looks like."

"This steak is really fabulous," said Hunter. "It's very tender and has some kind of spices on it. I don't know what they put on it to make it so delicious," said Hunter, egging Bill on. "It's a very fine piece of meat, too."

Hunter cut off a piece of steak and plopped it in his mouth. Bill watched him, hungrily.

"This has to be one of the best breakfasts I've ever had," said Hunter. "Why don't you forget about your French toast and order some steak and eggs? Nobody on the ship cares if you don't finish your French toast."

"No," said Bill. "I ordered French toast and I'm gonna stick with it. Your steak and eggs does look good, though. I haven't had steak and eggs for ages, not since I was a kid, come to think of it. And those hash browned potatoes look great, too."

"Are you sure you don't want to get an order?" asked Hunter. "You look to me like a steak and potatoes kind of man, if you don't mind my saying so."

Bill took what looked like a reluctant bite of his French toast.

"This French toast is pretty good," he said. "Everything on the ship is good. I should have known that and ordered the steak and eggs special. I'm kicking myself for not doing so. Of course, it's all your fault. If you hadn't ordered it, I never would have known what I was missing."

Mabel, meanwhile, had been staring intently at Hunter. He was wearing some clothes the captain had sent him—a *Royal Duchess* sweatshirt and a pair of slacks from one of the ship's stores.

"Solomon," she said, "I don't often encounter a person with as strong and as well defined an aura as yours, so even though I'm on vacation and have turned off my psychic powers, I couldn't help but get some messages about you. You are, I believe, a very intelligent person. You've got a good head on your shoulders, and you have a lot of imagination and fortitude. You're involved with making sure that things are done right, with making sure that people don't do anything they shouldn't do."

"Isn't this interesting?" thought Hunter.

"I get that sense from you," said Mabel. "I haven't come across anyone like you since I met my sister-in-law's boyfriend, Lance Killroy, from the Modesto Killroys. His father, Bruce, was head mechanic at the Ford garage, there. He married Betty Armstrong, his high school sweetheart. They went to Central High, if I recall correctly. Seems like lots of kids from Central High got married after they graduated. A lot of the girls were pregnant, too, when they got married, sad to say. But they weren't shotgun marriages, not by any means—except, that is, in a few of the cases. It always gives me a lot of pleasure when high school sweethearts get married. It means that they really know one another and don't have to worry about suddenly discovering unpleasant things about their spouses once they're married. Bill was my high school sweetheart, too. But I wasn't pregnant when we got married. We both went to Lincoln High in Gilroy. That's the place where they have those fantastic garlic festivals. I'm not much for garlic, mind you, but they've got a hundred different ways to cook garlic. Garlic jam, garlic pickles, roast garlic. You name it. Everything but garlic perfume, and they may be working on that. Gilroy's a nice town, but it has been changing in recent years, and not for the better. That's why I like living in Weed, which is where we moved once Bill retired from PG & E. We were always careful with our money and managed to save enough so we can live comfortably. And I make a bit with my psychic readings, too. We like Weed because it's high up and the air is clean, not like the valley, where the air is full of pesti-cides and poison."

Mabel stopped talking.

"Good Lord, I've been running off at the mouth and haven't fin-ished your reading. Like I said, you've got a good head on your shoul-ders and are a patient man, who waits for the right moment to do things. That tells me you can plan for the future and formulate your plans care-fully. I can sense that you're a professional man of some kind."

Mabel paused again and closed her eyes.

"Yes, yes, I'm getting a message," she said. "I don't usually try to guess what people do, but I'd say . . . I'd say, and tell me if I'm wrong, I'd say you're a professional man. But you're not snooty enough to be a doc-tor or a lawyer. So I'd say you're . . . you're an accountant!"

Hunter laughed.

"That was a good try, Mabel," he said. "You're pretty close. Let's just say that I'm a civil servant for the city of San Francisco. We can leave it at that."

Mabel had closed her eyes. "That's curious. I'm getting more messages," she said. "I see dark clouds; I sense danger. Maybe even death. The angel of death is hovering over this ship. Someone you know is in danger. Something terrible may happen."

She opened her eyes.

"I can't explain it," she said, "but all of a sudden these ominous images flooded into my head. I'm probably letting my imagination run wild. My stomach is a bit upset. Maybe that's what's behind those scary images."

"Perhaps," said Hunter.

A waiter came over to check on things.

"Did you enjoy your breakfast?" he asked.

"Say," said Bill, "do you think you could get me a half order of steak and eggs? This gentleman's breakfast looked so good I thought I'd try it, even though I've had some French toast."

"Very fine, sir," said the waiter. "A half order it is. And you, sir," he said, speaking to Hunter, "would you like another cappuccino?"

"I've had quite enough. I think I'd better walk around a bit and work off my breakfast."

"You're caught in a vicious cycle," said Bill. "Don't you see it? You got so much exercise this morning, walking around the deck, that you worked up a big appetite, and so you had that huge steak and eggs breakfast. Then you ate so much you decided that you've got to go back on that deck and work it off. After you do that and get more exercise, you'll be hungry again and will want a big lunch and after that you'll have to go back to the deck and work it off, to get ready for dinner. I wouldn't be surprised at all if you spent most of the cruise just doing two things—eating big meals in the Palm Court and walking around the deck in between meals."

"Isn't that, more or less, what everyone on this cruise is doing?" said Hunter. "Except that most of the passengers on the ship aren't doing much walking. Thanks for a most remarkable conversation."

With that he got up and left the Palm Court dining room. As he left he overheard Mabel whispering to her husband, "I still think he's an accountant. Just didn't want to admit it!"

Robert Musil, *The Man without Qualities*

Raymond Rogers,
*Coming into Existence:
The Struggle to
Become an Individual*

At this moment he wished to be a man without qualities. But this is probably not so different from what other people sometimes feel too. After all, by the time they have reached the middle of their life's journey few people remember how they have managed to arrive at themselves, at their amusements, their point of view, their wife, character, occupation and successes, but they cannot help feeling that not much is likely to change any more. It might even be asserted that they have been cheated, for one can nowhere discover any sufficient reason for everything's having come about as it has. It might just as well have turned out differently. The events of people's lives have, after all, only to the least degree originated in them, having generally depended on all sorts of circumstances such as the moods, the life or death of quite different people, and have, as it were, only at the given point of time come hurrying towards them. Something has had its way with them like a flypaper with a fly; it has caught them fast, here catching a little hair, there hampering their movements, and has gradually enveloped them, until they lie, buried under a thick coating that has only the remotest resemblance to their original shape. (151)

The line of investigation we've been pursuing provides a background of meaning for our original observation that the self is not born alone, into a psychic vacuum. It now seems beyond question that the self does not come into existence all by itself. The self comes into existence *just because* it becomes related to the other parts of the given. It is self-perceived, self-experienced, *in terms of* its relations to the other parts of the given. It is psychically located, or identified, *by means of* its relations to the other parts of the given. And the most important of these identifying relations are the ones established with other people: "to be is to be related." (36)

chapter **ten**

The Problematic of Postmodern Identity

Hunter decided to find something to read and made his way to the ship's library—a good-sized room with books in glass cabinets and an honor-system of sign-out sheets for the books. There were several people looking at books, and he could see that some people had signed out for books. After looking for a while he chose one by Thomas Pynchon, an American author, *The Crying of Lot 49*. He signed out for it and went looking for a quiet place to read it.

He walked up the stairs to the Lido Deck and sat down on a deck chair. He adjusted the back of the deck chair and was just about to start reading his book when Jean-Marie Benetton walked over and sat down on the next deck chair.

"Solomon," he said. "How nice to see you. Did you have a good breakfast?"

"Yes, indeed. A very interesting one," said Hunter. "I was at a table with a woman who told me she was a psychic. She was a very strange lady, and her husband was equally odd. She said she was going to tell me something about myself and then started rambling on and on and eventually forgot why she started talking."

"Scratch the ordinary person, and you find the same thing. Most people have their eccentricities and bizarre notions. That's what I've found," said Benetton. "They find ways to keep them hidden, but in certain situations they reveal themselves."

He was carrying a slender book.

"What are you reading?" asked Hunter.

"A most unusual book, maybe even a crazy one. It's called *Durkheim Is Dead,* and it's by an author from San Francisco named Berger. Ever heard of him?"

"No," said Hunter.

"He's not known in France, though I understand he has a small following in the United States. I wouldn't describe him as an important thinker, not at all. Very minor. A writer, I'd say from what I've read of this book, of literary curiosities that have a vague and rather superficial intellectual tinge to them and reflect a rather strong animosity towards professors and academic institutions. He teaches at a second- or third-tier school, San Francisco State University, so you wouldn't expect anything really first-rate from him. This book is, I'd say, a postmodern work—combining a mystery story, quotations from sociologists and social scientists, and a discussion of sociological theory. Quite strange. Bizarre."

"Is it a murder mystery?"

"A mystery, yes, but not a murder mystery," replied Benetton. "A friend of mine from Paris, Jean-Marie Benoist, wrote a book, *Marx est mort,* about the death of Marxism as a viable political philosophy. So when I saw this book, *Durkheim Is Dead,* I was intrigued. I didn't look at it carefully and thought, from the title, that it would be a sociological treatise on the end of Durkheim's influence on sociological thought, something like that.

"Instead, I have this wacky book in which Max Weber, a famous German sociologist, punches Emile Durkheim, the great French sociologist, in the nose at a party. As a result of this altercation, an elderly rich lady at the party faints, and a jewel she was wearing on a necklace disappears. At the party, which was organized by Weber's wife, Marianne, in addition to Durkheim and Weber, were a second German sociologist named Georg Simmel, Sigmund Freud, Vladimir Lenin, W. E. B. Du Bois, and a prominent English feminist thinker named Beatrice Webb. They had all come to London to give speeches at a conference. It turns out that in actuality, all of these people were alive in 1910, when the story takes place. So Sherlock Holmes is brought in to find the jewel and avoid a scandal. He interrogates everyone at the party. A good deal of the dialogue involves each person's theories about society and politics, so it's hard to say whether it is a mystery that's part sociology text or a sociology text that's part mystery. It also is an imitation Sherlock Holmes novel, so it's very hard to classify."

"I've read other imitation Sherlock Holmes mysteries," said Hunter. "There are quite a few of them."

"Yes," said Benetton. "The existence of these books shows the centrality of the matter of identity, which I and my colleagues are working on. You see, matters and questions involving identity are everywhere, though the average person doesn't think about identity or recognize it to be a problematic. I am a sociologist and a particular kind of one—I am what is known as a postmodernist."

"I've heard the term and actually met some postmodernists a number of years ago, if I recall correctly," said Hunter. "But they all seemed to disagree with one another on what postmodernism was, so I never really got clear on the matter. What kind are you?"

Benetton laughed.

"You must recognize, Hunter, that academics, by nature and training, are inclined to disagree with one another and spend their lives trying to prove that their ideas are right and everyone else's ideas are wrong. Every academic believes that his or her field is central and his or her perspective on the field is the right one."

"So—what's your take on postmodernism?" asked Hunter. "And how does it explain the matter of identity? I've already heard a good deal about identity from your colleagues. I'd never thought too much about it before, as I said earlier."

"If there is anything fundamental to postmodernism it's that the old philosophical systems no longer are convincing to people," said

Benetton. "We no longer believe in the old great narratives that explained life to most of us, and so everything is in flux, including identity. Identity used to be based on the notion of stability and sameness. People developed an identity, and it was thought to be a true reflection of their character and personality. There was what might be called an element of sameness to people. Of course, people change as they grow older, and some people have experiences—such as in battle—that may have profound impacts on them, but even though they are older, they generally aren't radically different from what they were like earlier."

"That makes sense to me," said Hunter.

"Until around 1960, our culture could be described as modernist. We built buildings that were slabs of glass and concrete and believed in reason and logic. We thought that by using reason and logic, we would inevitably make life better for people. That all crashed around 1960 when the postmodernist mentality suddenly took over—what might be called a cultural mutation. Suddenly, things were different. For example, the notion that elite culture was different and better than popular culture was a modernist notion. In postmodernism, the differences between elite and popular culture are erased. Anything goes. Postmodernist culture is ironic and loves to play games. It revels in superficiality and is eclectic. The world of media and images now is dominant, and simulations and imitations are fashionable. So when it comes to identity, we no longer expect sameness, continuity, and coherence. People are free to switch their identities as often as they wish, which they do by changing the signs that we all use to announce to others who and what we are. I believe Anastasia explained that to you when you had your talk."

"Yes," said Hunter. "She told me about her work with signs and said that people are always sending messages to one another by the way they dress, their hair color, their hairstyles. Just about everything they do. I found our chat most instructive. I can imagine that men would go wild over Anastasia, with that beautiful blonde hair and wonderful figure."

"Some people say she's got ahead because she's so beautiful and uses her good looks most effectively. Marshall McInnis was smitten by her. He had what you Americans call a relationship with Katarina and, so I've heard, suddenly abandoned her to chase after Anastasia. What he didn't realize is that his energy was misdirected. Of course, he didn't live to find this out."

"What do you mean?" asked Hunter.

"Anastasia is one of the sisterhood, from Lesbos. She's a lesbian!" said Benetton.

"That's hard to believe," replied Hunter.

"Beautiful women can be lesbians," added Benetton. "Many are. And do you know who Anastasia has fallen in love with?" he asked.

"I would guess that since Katarina and Anastasia are on the outs, it would have to be either Antonia or Symphonie," said Hunter. "Unless you and Sigfried are women."

"You're got a good head," said Benetton. "I can see that you're very quick. Yes, it would be either Antonia or Symphonie, and it happens to be Symphonie. But Symphonie loves me, posing considerable problems for Anastasia."

"I can see that professors lead very complicated lives. Of course, since everyone's a postmodernist nowadays, you can't be sure how long your relationship with Symphonie will last and whether Anastasia will decide to stop being a lesbian and focus her attention on members of the opposite sex. Wouldn't that be possible?"

"Yes, of course," said Benetton. "You'll learn more about women and identity when you have your conversation with Symphonie."

Hunter noticed that Benetton had a dreamy look on his face.

"She's also a beautiful woman, isn't she?" said Hunter.

"Yes, yes," said Benetton. "Very beautiful. Many Asian women are. And lately they've begun to recognize it. I call them Suzie Wongs. There are many strikingly beautiful Asian women. Suddenly, Asian women have become fashionable."

"Have you known her long?" asked Hunter.

"Not at all," said Benetton. "We had met at conferences from time to time over the years, but it is only since we've been together on this cruise that we've been able to spend a lot of time together and I've really got to know her. When I first met her, I found her quite reserved and only interested in talking about scholarly matters. She was a kind of hyperintellectual. Now, she's more relaxed and seems reluctant to talk about her work or anything of an intellectual nature. She probably over-did it and decided her scholarly personality wasn't satisfactory, so she changed. People do as they get older. Now she wants to have fun."

"She was married to McInnis for a while, I understand," said Hunter.

"Yes, and it was terrible for her. Maybe that's why she's changed. She said he was a monster. He was affable when with others, but he had a false persona. The word means mask, you know. So people thought of him as friendly and witty, but he treated Symphonie like dirt. He was un-faithful to her, and he beat her. When I think of that, I get so angry with him that I could . . ."

He paused.

"It is not good to speak ill of the dead," he said. "As terrible a person as he was, I still feel sorry for him, dying of that heart attack. Very sad."

Hunter decided to switch the subject.

"Let me ask a question related to this matter of identity. Sym-phonie has beautiful, shiny black hair. Isn't that a stable aspect of her identity?" asked Hunter.

"Until she decides to see what life is like as a blonde or a red-head or a brunette," he replied. "Have you noticed that many Asian women and other women of color have started dyeing their hair? Some 'wild' Japanese women dyed their hair brown a few years ago. And now there are many Japanese blondes."

"I see," said Hunter. "So it's postmodernism that explains this?"

"Yes," replied Benetton. "Of course, Symphonie might decide to dye her hair purple or cut all her hair off. In postmodern societies like America, people change their hair colors, their dress, their jobs, and, as you pointed out, their lovers, without seeming to think twice about it. There's nothing that's really stable about our identities. If you're a brunette, you can become a blonde. If you're a man, you can dress like a woman and vice versa. Or even become one. You can be a ditchdigger and pretend to be a surgeon, or a waitress and pretend to be an opera star. Identity is up for grabs in postmodern societies."

He stopped for a moment and then laughed.

"You know," he said, "Marx actually said something that strikes me as very postmodern. He wrote that under communism it will be possible to do one thing today and something else tomorrow, to hunt in the morning, fish in the afternoon, rear cattle in the evening, and criticize after dinner, without ever becoming a hunter, fisherman, rancher, or critic. Marx anticipated, one might say, certain aspects of postmodernism, as far as lifestyles are concerned. A famous postmodernist thinker, Jean-François Lyotard, once explained how eclecticism is an important element of postmodern life. You listen to reggae, then later you watch a western; you have a McDonald's hamburger for lunch and local cuisine for dinner; you wear retro clothes in Hong Kong and French perfume in Tokyo. And the only value of knowledge is to win prizes on television game shows. Everything is mixed up whatever way you want it. You can see it most directly in postmodern architecture, which uses a number of different styles in one building. The basic metaphor in postmodernism is the pastiche, the mixture of styles, and, in our everyday lives, lifestyles."

"So for postmodernists there's no constant to identity, or to anything?" asked Hunter.

"No constant except constant change and the value of the dollar bill or Euro," said Benetton. "When you look for a constant in identity, you reveal yourself as a modernist. But, of course, you were raised in modernist times. Your age tells me that you didn't grow up in the sixties or seventies. What happened, as I suggested earlier, was that there was a major cultural shift or mutation around 1960 and suddenly things changed. These changes affected young people who were growing up at the time when postmodernism had started asserting itself. So people in their forties and younger generations were raised in postmodern times and were affected by it. Postmodernism isn't simply a philosophical perspective that is debated by professors. It shapes contemporary consciousness, which is media driven and full of simulations and imitations—what one French philosopher, Baudrillard, called hyperreality."

At this moment, Symphonie walked by.

"Hello, Solomon," she said. "Nice to see you again." She flashed a smile. Then she spoke to Jean-Marie Benetton.

"I've been looking all over for you. Let's take a walk and then get a drink."

She noticed he was carrying *Durkheim Is Dead*.

"You can read that silly mystery later. There's always time for books!"

"Yes, let's take a walk around the deck. That's a good idea," said Benetton. "If you'll excuse me, Solomon. I enjoyed our chat, but I cannot resist the call of this siren."

He got up, kissed Symphonie on the cheek, and walked off with her.

Hunter sat in his deck chair, thinking for a few minutes. There was a lot of information to digest, and he was trying to make sense of what he had learned. McInnis had been married to Wu for a short period of time. She might harbor a deep hatred for him. Did she leave him, or could it have been the other way around? And McInnis had dumped Katarina Mittags to chase after Anastasia, who had been described as having round heels for men who could help her but also, by someone else, as a lesbian or a bisexual. So there were two women who might despise McInnis. But enough to want to kill him? Even in a postmodern world, you don't kill someone without a motive. Or do you?

He took the book he had borrowed from the ship's library, opened it up, and started reading: *One summer afternoon Mrs. Oedipa Maas came home from a Tupperware party whose hostess had put perhaps too much kirsch in the fondue to find that she, Oedipa, had been named executor, or she supposed, executrix . . .*

What matters to people is how they should live with other people. The great questions of social life are "Who am I?" (To what kind of a group do I belong?) and "What should I do?" (Are there many or few prescriptions I am expected to obey?). Groups are strong or weak according to whether they have boundaries separating them from others. Decisions are taken either for the group as a whole (strong boundaries) or for individuals or families (weak boundaries). Prescriptions are few or many indicating the individual internalizes a large or a small number of behavioral norms to which he or she is bound. By combining boundaries with prescriptions . . . the most general answers to the questions of social life can be combined to form four different political cultures. Strong groups with numerous prescriptions that vary with social roles combine to form hierarchical collectivism. Strong groups whose members follow few prescriptions form an egalitarian culture, a shared life of voluntary consent, without coercion or inequality. Competitive individualism joins few prescriptions with weak boundaries, thereby encouraging ever new combinations. When groups are weak and prescriptions strong, so that decisions are made for them by people on the outside, the controlled culture is fatalistic. (7)

Aaron Wildavsky, "Conditions for a Pluralist Democracy, or Cultural Pluralism Means More Than One Political Culture in a Country"

Gordon W. Allport, *Becoming: Basic Considerations for a Psychology of Personality*

The Leibnitzian tradition . . . maintains that the person is not a collection of acts, nor simply the locus of acts; the person is the *source* of acts. And activity itself is not conceived as agitation resulting from pushes by internal or external stimulation. It is purposive. To understand what a person is, it is necessary always to refer to what he may be in the future, for every state of the person is pointed in the direction of future possibilities. (12)

chapter **eleven**

Katarina Mittags

After lunch Talcott Weems went to see what the art auction was like and Solomon Hunter decided to take a stroll around the ship, hoping he might find someone from the identity group to talk with. In the Plaza Lounge he noticed Katarina Mittags sitting by herself, having a drink. She had a glum look on her face.

"May I join you?" he asked. "I see you're all by yourself. Perhaps you'd like a bit of company?"

"Yes, yes, of course," replied Katarina.

Hunter noticed that there seemed to be a slight hesitancy to her voice, as if she really didn't want to be with anyone but was too polite to say so. Or, perhaps, she was expecting someone?

"How are you enjoying the cruise?" Hunter asked.

"For a person in my field—there's a strong element of the social anthropologist in my makeup—this cruise is a truly remarkable opportunity. It's like being suddenly parachuted into a nontraditional, what most people would call 'primitive,' culture somewhere and trying to figure out what's going on. There's a whole little world contained in this ship, with all kinds of interesting things going on that anyone with any degree of intellectual curiosity would find most curious and would want to figure out. It's a big surprise, I must say. I might even do some writing about cruising when I'm done with this identity project. There's a lot of interest in tourism now in the academic world, but almost nothing has been written about cruises that I can recall seeing. Of course, I never looked for anything on them, but you notice books that are published and that kind of thing."

Hunter noticed that she had now become quite animated.

"How is your work on the identity project progressing?" inquired Hunter.

"Very well, thank you. You see, as a social anthropologist, we study the way social structures shape culture. *Culture* is the big word in academia nowadays. It has replaced society and even class, though I'm kidded, all the time, about being a Marxist because I believe in the importance of class. But in a special way."

"I've met some Marxists in my day," said Hunter. "Most of them seem to me to be quite doctrinaire. They seem to have pat answers for every problem. Everything boils down to false consciousness, imperialism, alienation, and a couple of other things. I must say I find it all tedious. I had a chat with Jean-Marie Benetton, who told me a friend of his in France wrote a book called *Marxism est mort*. I guess a lot of people feel the same way I do."

Katarina smiled.

"Every generation buries Marx, only to resurrect him when people need explanations for what's going on in their societies. I would argue, in a manner similar to Marx, that an individual in a group seldom is aware of what might be called the prevailing ideas and styles of thought in the group that shape his or her thinking. Perhaps dominate that thinking is a better word. For example, I've done some work on what might be called political cultures and lifestyles. I've used ideas I got from a British social anthropologist, Mary Douglas, and an American political scientist, Aaron Wildavsky."

She paused for a moment.

"Is this boring you?" she asked.

"Not at all," said Hunter.

"Good," said Katarina. "I don't want to talk about this if you're not interested in it. What they suggest is that in every society, people want to know two things—who they are and what they should do. That is, what their identity is and how they should behave. People deal with the question of their identities by belonging either to strong groups that make decisions that are binding on everyone or weak groups that allow people to choose which rules to obey and which to neglect. They solve the problem of action by becoming members of a group that has many rules or few rules. Thus, there are two dominant variables: the strength or weakness of group boundaries and the number and variety of group prescriptions. If you consider the possibilities of weak and strong boundaries and many or few prescriptions, you end up with four political cultures, or, in more general terms, lifestyles—what Wildavsky called elitists, individualists, egalitarians, and fatalists."

"I see," said Hunter.

"Are you following me?" she asked.

"Yes," said Hunter. "And I'm wondering which of those lifestyles I belong to. I'd never thought of society in those terms."

"Sometimes he changed the words he used, but for all practical purposes, these four are the only political cultures found in democratic societies."

"I'm with you. So far so good," said Hunter.

"Good," she replied. "Now when we attach ourselves to one of the four groups, we don't do this consciously. We just know that certain things seem basic or crucial to us and so we end up either as elitists, who believe that hierarchy is important; or individualists, who think government should just protect property and do little else; or egalitarians, who stress that everyone has certain needs and want to use the government to uplift the downtrodden, namely the fatalists, who are the bottom of the heap. My argument, then, is that it is membership in these groups that shapes people's identities. We are, after all, social animals, and our identities, it could be said, are socially conferred and are based on our being a member of one of these four groups—even though we may not recognize that such is the case."

A waiter came over, and Hunter ordered a double Scotch on the rocks.

"People may not be conscious that they are in one culture or another," she continued, "but they do recognize that they have certain core beliefs and values and that there are other people who are like them in terms of their beliefs. They seek reinforcement in works in the media and popular culture for their beliefs and avoid works that cause dissonance and run counter to their beliefs. Marxists would explain these groups as follows. They would see the elitists as the bourgeoisie, the ruling class, whose ideas become the ideas of the working classes. The individualists would be what a Marxist would call petit bourgeois, small businessmen who are very conservative and terrified of losing status. Egalitarians are close to Marxists in that they stress the needs all people have, though they don't believe in things like the dictatorship of the proletariat that some Marxists believe in. And finally the fatalists would be the proletariat—those who have nothing to sell except their labor—who have little consciousness of their condition. And whose only chance of rising is a matter of luck—winning a lottery or something like that.

"When people buy things, they do so as members of one of these four cultures, each of which, you must realize, feels antagonistic toward the three other cultures. Shopping, then, becomes, in a curious way, a political statement. It is a reflection of one's lifestyle. Some culture critics talk about America as a consumer culture, but they are too simplistic. There are, as Mary Douglas's theory explains, four consumer cultures in the United States and all advanced industrial nations. That means, for example, that the passengers who chose to take this cruise line did so because they thought it was the kind of line that people like them would also take. They expected to find 'their kind of people' on this cruise and not other kinds of people—those from other consumer cultures."

She paused.

"That's most interesting," said Hunter. "I never would have thought of shopping as a kind of political statement or of their being so many different kinds of consumers."

"I'm afraid we're not having a conversation, but I'm giving you a lecture on social anthropology. It's what I was writing about this morning, so it's fresh in my head. I hope you'll forgive me."

"This cruise is turning out to be much more stimulating than I thought it would. Too bad cruise companies don't schedule more professors like you to teach passengers about various topics, so cruises would be more interesting for those with intellectual interests and who want to learn about various topics," said Hunter.

"Actually, that's not a bad idea," said Katarina. "Marshall would have been very good at that sort of thing. He used jazzy phrases to give people things to think about and capture their imaginations. He was also very funny at times. He had the ability to reach the common person."

"You're doing quite well, yourself," said Hunter.

Katarina blushed.

"You're quite a gentleman," she said. "You know we're all trying to figure you out. We're all interested in identity, as you well know, as an academic subject. But on the personal level we feel that there's something rather mysterious about you. I can't put my finger on it, but we all feel there's more to you than you let on. You're an enigma, an unclassifiable image, Solomon. No doubt about that!"

"Not just a wise guy, but an enigma," he joked. "Tell me, how did you get involved with this project?"

"I assume someone has told you this already, but maybe not? Marshall and I were sleeping together, when we could arrange to be together, that is. I was under the impression that we were going to get married. It was easy for Marshall to arrange lectures where I teach. And I spent summers in the United States, in Los Angeles, where he taught. He said he would make what you Americans call an 'honest' woman out of me and talked about eloping to Las Vegas. Then, a while ago, he went to Bologna to give a lecture, got involved with Anastasia, and my life started unraveling. He always had an eye for other women. I knew that, but, fool that I was, I thought I could hold on to him. The next thing I knew he started slipping away from me. I was furious with him and with Anastasia, as well."

Hunter looked at Katarina. Her eyes were flashing and her face was frozen, for just an instant, in hate.

"If Marshall McInnis is dead and Sigfried is too old—at least I would imagine he's too old to be of interest to Anastasia—I guess that leaves Jean-Marie to be her next conquest," said Hunter.

"Jean-Marie is preoccupied with his postmodernism nonsense and with Symphonie Wu," said Katarina. "She's also a very beautiful woman, so Anastasia probably will have to find someone else to amuse her during the cruise. It won't be difficult for her, no doubt. She has a lot of experience with that kind of thing. It might be the captain of the ship, or even you. You never can tell. Everyone's vulnerable when you have a dangerous woman like Anastasia on the loose."

"What can you tell me about Symphonie?" asked Hunter. "Jean-Marie said she used to be quite reserved and now seems a bit different."

"Yes, that's true. Everyone used to call Symphonie the 'porcelain maiden.' She was beautiful and dedicated, but there was something about her that bothered people. She was always reserved, very intellectual, and very distant. You always had the feeling that if you touched her by accident she might crack into a thousand pieces. Now, I take it, she's more relaxed. That often happens when you get tenure or are promoted to full professor. Some scholars, when they become full professors, never do another thing of academic significance. They just coast until they retire. Probably because they got burned out getting there. Being a professor isn't an easy life. People don't realize that."

"I've chatted with Anastasia and with Antonia and now with you, but nobody has said anything about Sigfried Duerfklein. How does he fit into your group?"

"Sigfried is a sweet old man. He's very kindly and gentle and a prolific writer," said Katarina. "He can write on anything because he has a methodology that enables him to analyze anything and everything— psychoanalytic theory. All Sigfried does is write about sex, and all I do is think about it! That's the problem with Freudians. Everything, in the final analysis, ends up involving sex and Freud's mythical Oedipus complex. But Sigfried, fortunately, has an imagination and doesn't take himself too seriously. He wrote a classic work on identity, *The Secret Self: The Psychology of the Impostor*. When you talk with him, he'll explain it. In short, he argues that everyone is an impostor and that we keep our real selves hidden, and do it so well that we don't know who or what we are. Even Michiko Kakutani at the *New York Times* liked the book."

"That doesn't happen very often, does it?" said Hunter.

"Hardly ever. She's a tough reviewer," said Katarina. "Fortunately, she didn't review my latest book, *The Social Self*. I make the argument in it that I told you about. I must admit to being heavily influenced by the French sociologist Durkheim, who argued that people are, in a sense, split into two selves; people are in society, and society is in people. We internalize the rules society teaches us and don't recognize the extent to which society shapes our behavior. Durkheim, you have to realize, had important things to say about identity. He suggested that society is present in individuals, who internalize its rules of conduct and morality."

"Durkheim again!" said Hunter. "Jean-Marie was reading something about Durkheim."

"Is that so? How interesting!" replied Katarina. "Do you recall what its title was?"

"If I remember correctly it was called *Durkheim's Death* or *Durkheim Is Dead*. He said it was a Sherlock Holmes mystery in which

Max Weber punched Durkheim in the nose. He thought it a strange book."

Katarina laughed.

"Strange, indeed. I've read it. I would have to describe it as an unconventional work, to put it mildly. I found it mildly fascinating. The author has Sherlock Holmes interview a number of famous sociologists and thinkers, including Freud, no less, who seems to be the star of the show. In the book we find Sherlock Holmes uttering stupid lines like 'This digs deep, Watson' to make readers think they're reading a real Sherlock Holmes story. In essence it's a primer—an elementary and somewhat simpleminded textbook on sociological theory disguised as a Sherlock Holmes mystery. I'm astounded that anyone would publish such a bit of nonsense, or that Jean-Marie would read it. Sigfried would explain it as one more example of the lack of authenticity in society and of the dominance of duplicity. He'd say that the book is a fake Sherlock Holmes book and the author is an impostor."

"But you read it," said Hunter.

"Yes, but I read everything I can lay my hands on about Durkheim, so I have an excuse. The author is, I believe, a charlatan. I think he's putting on everyone, and getting away with it to boot. I imagine Jean-Marie said it was postmodern and therefore a contribution to understanding contemporary life and culture. The problem with postmodernism is that anything can be described that way. Postmodern theories of identity are nonsensical because postmodernism is nonsense. It is, in the final analysis, whatever you want it to be. But don't get me started on postmodernism! My lecture on that runs for two hours, at the very least."

At that moment, Sigfried Duerfklein appeared.

"Katarina. It's time for the dance lesson in the Stage Door Lounge. We must leave or we'll be late," he said. "It's Latin dancing. We'll learn how to do the cha-cha-cha and maybe the tango?"

"Yes," said Katarina, turning to Hunter. "We both love to dance. Would you care to join us?"

"No thanks," said Hunter. "I think I'll just stay here for a while and take it easy."

Katarina and Sigfried walked off, heading to the Stage Door Lounge, and Hunter sat, thinking about what he had learned. "I'm getting quite an education, but am I getting any closer to finding out who killed Marshall McInnis?" he wondered.

Orrin E. Klapp, *The Collective Search for Identity*

Raymond Rogers, *Coming into Existence: The Struggle to Become an Individual*

A society fails to supply adequate identity when symbols are disturbed to the extent that they no longer give reliable reference points (in such things as status symbols, place symbols, style models, cultic values, mystiques) by which people can locate themselves socially, realize themselves sentimentally, and declare (to self and others) who they are. We now live in a world in which catastrophic changes are occurring in reference symbols, yet the notion persists that you can change a man's style, teach him new languages and a new religion, run tractors under his window wiping out a landscape, and he will still be the same man—with a little sophistication added perhaps. (viii)

A belief evolving from an attitude which was generated unreflectingly in action can be said simply to happen, to occur by chance. This way of arriving at convictions is in sharp contrast to the self-examining method of carving them out with care and deliberation. We have noted earlier that some of our assumptions are accepted by chance from other people, and we are now adding to that there is another accidental way to acquire them. . . . They are created by activities we just happen to undertake, by dynamic unifications worked out to solve problems we happen to encounter. Some of these randomly created premises help to form the very foundations of our self-structures, just as the randomly inherited ones do. . . . Enter any activity unthinkingly and it shapes you. Or, more accurately, you shape yourself just as surely by your unthinking activities as you do by your thinking. Even in the absence of awareness, that is, self-activity is active rather than passive. When it is later remembered or called into awareness, however, self-activity that occurred without awareness has the subtle flavor and feel of something that simply happened. (85–86)

chapter **twelve**

Tea without Sympathy

Talcott Weems had studied the *Duchess Daily* carefully and discovered that tea was served in the Palm Court from 3:30 to 4:30 p.m.

"Come on, Solly," he said, "let's go to afternoon tea and see who we meet. Lunch was a real hoot. I never realized there were so many weird people floating around outside the nuthouses."

"Why not?" said Hunter. "I can use a bit of diversion. Chatting with these professors is really demanding. They're all pretty passionate about their ideas, and I have to work really hard to follow them when they're explaining their theories. That's because, at the same time, I'm looking for information that will help us with the investigation."

Hunter and Weems walked down to the Palm Court dining room. A small band was playing music. About a hundred people were sitting around tables while waiters with white gloves poured tea and other waiters brought platters full of small sandwiches and little cakes. One waiter had a paper bag in which there were hot scones.

A waiter brought them to a large round table that was empty and seated them.

101

"So this is how the classy people live," said Weems. "I could get used to it."

They had no sooner sat down when another waiter brought a passenger over, and the man sat down next to Hunter. The man was about fifty. He had a scraggly beard, beady eyes, and a nose that seemed to veer off to the left of his face. He had a diamond stud in his right ear. Several waiters suddenly appeared and poured tea and offered them things to eat.

"Good afternoon," he said. "This looks like a pleasant way to spend an hour—having tea and good things to eat."

"Yes," said Hunter.

"My wife might be coming to join us in a little while," the man said. "She's at the spa. God only knows what they're doing to her down there. And it's costing me a small fortune, as well. Things add up on this ship. Between the drinks, the spa, the souvenirs, and the tours, this cruise is costing me a lot of money. You have to be careful about these side expenses. But the tea is free, so that's something, at least."

Hunter laughed.

"My name is Solomon Hunter," he said, "and this gentleman next to me is Talcott Weems. Pleased to make your acquaintance."

"Talbot Parsons's my name," he said. "This is my first cruise. It's a fascinating experience. The sociologist in me makes me think cruises are worth investigating."

"You an academic?" asked Weems. "Not again," he was thinking. "I can't get away from these damned professors."

"Used to be," said Parsons. "Taught at Southwest Missouri State University for a number of years. My wife also taught there—that's where I met her. We wrote an introduction to sociology textbook—Parsons and Parsons's *The Sociological Perspective*. It's now in its eighth edition. We both retired early and became writers. Now my wife, Talula, and I spend our lives rewriting the book. It's boring as hell, but it pays the bills. You have to make the book boring enough for professors, who think if a book is tedious and dreary, it must be good. Sort of like eating mashed potatoes without any salt or butter. And you have to bring out a new edition every three years or else your sales crash since students don't keep books anymore. They sell them to bookstores as soon as they've taken their final examinations. The bookstores keep reselling them and raking in the dough. And writers only get royalties when the book is sold the first time."

"You'll be interested to know there are a number of other professors on this cruise," said Hunter. "We're assigned to sit with a group of them at dinner. They're involved in some kind of literary experiment. Each of them is writing a chapter on identity during the cruise. When they get back to San Francisco, they hope to put them together and have a book. They're all cultural studies scholars."

"Cultural studies is a lot of crap," said Parsons. "I think it was dreamed up by publishers. Books in cultural studies sell like crazy, for some reason. A lot of the people in cultural studies are English professors who couldn't find any students interested in taking seminars on Milton and that kind of thing. They wanted an excuse to write about film and photography and pop culture, so they latched on to cultural studies, which was dreamed up in Britain. Cultural studies is cutting into our sales a lot."

"I had no idea," said Hunter. "I've had a chat with a few of the professors at our table, and I found their ideas quite refreshing."

"Most of the stuff in cultural studies is garbage. It's about cross-dressing, lesbian, bisexual, transgender, and gay culture, sports, comic strips, video games—that kind of junk. What makes things worse is that editors keep on requesting more and more books in the field, if you can call it a field. More studies of Madonna. Maybe a scholarly analysis of Britney Spears will be next? Or Dick Tracy? And all that nonsense about postcolonialism. What's happened is that nobody talks about works of literature anymore. They just use literature, art, film, whatever, as an excuse for more ideological rantings and ravings. But students, being young and rebellious, eat the stuff up, and it sells. That's all that editors are interested in, you have to realize. People in cultural studies are like those poor souls with multiple personalities. This personality and you're a Marxist, that one and you're a sociologist. Another personality and you're a psychoanalytic critic. Next personality uses semiotics. In cultural studies, I often think the writers say 'round up the usual suspects' in terms of the disciplines they use, then run everything through their multidisciplinary template."

"You don't seem to have a very high opinion of professors or of editors," said Hunter. "I always thought it was very prestigious to be a professor and also to be an editor."

"If you only knew," said Parsons, taking a sip of tea and a bite of a sandwich. "Basically, as I see things, an editor's basic function is to take authors to lunch or, if you're a really important author from an Ivy League school, for example, to dinner at some expensive French restaurant. Editors fawn over scholars from big-name schools and treat everyone else like dirt. And they seem to take glee in rejecting manuscripts. They have, you must realize, just about absolute power when it comes to choosing manuscripts, though I suspect the real locus of power is in the marketing departments of publishers. If the marketing director likes a book and thinks it will sell, the acquisitions editor then will decide the book has merit and it probably will get published."

"I had no idea publishing was so difficult," said Hunter. "I've heard about publishing or perishing, but you make it sound like publishing and perishing are very similar."

"In academic publishing, which is what I'm talking about," said Parsons, "you have to realize that most editors don't know anything to speak of about the subject of a book, except what they pick up from handling manuscripts over the years and from talking with professors and looking over this or that prospectus for books.

"Many of them are egomaniacs. They only publish books that they've commissioned, books that were, they think, essentially their ideas, or ones that they worked on with an author. When you deal with editors, you have to find ways of convincing them that your idea was originally their idea. Then you have a chance of getting a manuscript published. When you deal with editors, there can be endless delays, while they leave your manuscript sitting on their desk for months. Then, they send it to so-called experts in the field who leave it sitting for another six months, or even longer in some cases. Then, after the editors hear from the reviewers, who generally hate to have anything published that they or one of their friends hasn't written, the editors give it a quick read and often reject it. But when editors want something from an author, then it's a different story. They want it done immediately. It's very aggravating."

"Then why do you bother with them, Professor Parsons?" asked Weems. "If editors are such bastards and publishing books is so aggravating, why not do something else?"

"There are three reasons," said Parsons. "The first is that publishing is, in the final analysis, a big ego trip. You have to have a certain amount of ego strength to write and to deal with editors. And with rejection. There are always problems, even with nice editors. But, then, there is a bit of a thrill you feel when a book of yours has been set into print and published. Your ideas will be spread, professors will assign your books, and students will read them. Perhaps it is more accurate to say that students will be assigned your books; most of the students probably won't bother, but a few will. It's always the idea of having a saving remnant. When I taught, there were always a few students who were interested and who read the assignments. So we write for those few who will read our books, hoping that others will, sooner or later. I doubt that anyone has ever read our sociology book without being forced to do so by a professor threatening quizzes and hour exams. That's what you face when you write textbooks."

"What was the second reason for writing, Professor Parsons?" Talcott asked. "You only told us one."

"Money! What else? We write because we want people to read what we've written, but we also need to make a living. Even with all the aggravations from editors, it's a hell of a lot better writing than teaching in a university. You don't have all those blasted boring committee meetings that drag on endlessly and never achieve closure. You don't have all those damned administrators bugging you and you don't have all those whiny students complaining about the grade you gave them on this or that paper or making endless excuses about why they'll be passing in a late paper or why they missed an exam. A large percentage of students are binge drinkers now. They go to class between binges. Why they bother going to college is beyond me."

He paused for a moment.

"You gentlemen aren't professors, by chance?" he asked.

"No," replied Hunter. "But we've had occasion to meet professors from time to time over the years, and as I said earlier, we're sitting with a bunch of them every evening. I find the conversation over dinner to be very stimulating and this matter of identity that they're working on quite a puzzle. I never realized there was so much to it."

"Just another academic fad, one more hot topic that will soon cool down," said Parsons. "All this cultural studies nonsense will fade away eventually, to be replaced by something equally silly. But introduction to sociology textbooks will go on forever."

A waiter came over and poured more tea. Another waiter, with hot scones in a paper bag, came and gave everyone scones.

"The third reason is that there's nothing else I can do to make a buck. And, despite it all, I love dealing with editors and publishing books," Parsons added. "The ink gets into your blood. I can't explain it."

"The ink gets into your blood, and you get to put the royalties into your bank account," said Weems. "Doesn't sound bad to me."

Parsons laughed.

"And remember those free lunches."

Erich Fromm, *Beyond the Chains of Illusion: My Encounter with Marx and Freud*

Hendrik M. Ruitenbeek, *The Individual and the Crowd: A Study of Identity in America*

The character structure determines action, as well as thoughts and ideas. Let us take a few examples: for the anal-hoarding character, the ideal of saving is most attractive and, in fact, he tends to regard saving as one of the major virtues. He will like a way of life in which saving is encouraged and waste prohibited. . . . A person with an oral-receptive character orientation feels "the source of all good" to be outside, and he believes that the only way to get what he wants—be it something material, be it affection, love, knowledge, pleasure—is to receive it from that outside source. In this orientation the problem of love is almost exclusively that of "being loved" and not that of loving. Such people tend to be indiscriminate in the choice of their love objects, because being loved by anybody is such an overwhelming experience for them that they "fall for" anybody who gives them love or what looks like love. They are exceedingly sensitive to any withdrawal or rebuff they experience on the part of the loved person. (74–75)

Many Americans no longer take anything at face value. Everything must have some inner meaning; everything, even the most idle remarks, must be interpreted. We have gone far beyond merely regarding slips of the tongue as "Freudian" and have become self-conscious about our most ordinary behavior. This self-consciousness may well contribute to anxiety and insecurity. Many a person is just sufficiently well acquainted with psychoanalytic thinking to know that what he says, and even what gestures he makes, can betray his "unconscious motives" to the alert and informed observer. Such a person, perhaps himself willing to jump to conclusions about others, may feel acutely aware that others are watching and appraising him in the light of their psychoanalytic knowledge, though that may be as scanty as his own. (65)

chapter **thirteen**

Sigfried Duerfklein

After tea, Weems went back to their stateroom to watch CNN and Hunter decided on another walk around the Sun Deck. He found Sigfried Duerfklein there, strolling in a leisurely manner and enjoying the lovely weather. He was wearing white sneakers and a green track-suit.

"Ah, Mr. Hunter," Duerfklein said, when he noticed Hunter. "I've heard you've been talking with my colleagues and getting an earful. Will you join me in walking around the deck? I need some fresh air. I love to look at the sea. It has a hypnotic power to it that has always aroused my curiosity."

"I'm having a good time with your colleagues. They're an unusually interesting group of people," said Hunter.

"Yes, quite so. Anastasia said you were very curious about her ideas, and about us. Just as we're curious about you. A matter of chance, perhaps, that you were seated at our table. But a serendipitous event for you, I would imagine, for now you're learning a great deal about identity."

"And about you and your colleagues as well," added Hunter. "People are naturally curious about those they meet, whether at a party

109

or at the dinner table on a cruise. And I must confess that I am, by nature, a very curious person. Very curious!"

"Yes, yes . . . of course," replied Duerfklein. "As I understand it,
you've had chats with everyone except Symphonie and me. Did you
learn anything interesting about me from your conversations with my
colleagues?"

"Sometimes, you have to realize," Hunter said, "you don't know
when something you've learned about something actually is interesting.
You only find that out later."

"Very true," said Duerfklein. "Very true. So I've discovered in my
work as a psychoanalyst."

"Antonia, I believe, said you were a very distinguished scholar,"
added Hunter. "And someone, I can't recall who, mentioned that you
have a fascinating theory about identity—namely that we're all impostors, or something like that."

Duerfklein laughed.

"Yes, impostors! That's the word. My theories really bother my
colleagues because they tend to look at human beings in aggregates, as
members of society or some class or culture or subculture. So they can
talk about things like behavior in crowds or American national character
and identity—whatever that might be—or various ideological positions
that still deal with large groups of people: women, gays, the proletariat.
You name it. My focus, since I have a psychoanalytic approach to things,
deals with individuals and how they achieve their identities. Or don't
achieve them, since many people, as my theory suggests, are pretenders
to an identity."

"I don't understand how that can happen." said Hunter.
"Jean-Marie said that in postmodern societies people often change
their identities to suit their whims, but that doesn't seem to me to
be the same thing as pretending to have an identity or being an impostor."

Duerfklein smiled, knowingly.

"Our personalities, from my perspective, are masks, which is what the Latin term *persona* means. So our personalities are, it can be said, masks that we create to deal with others in social situations. You might contrast one's personality with what might be called one's character or 'self,' one's true being. What I argue, based on my work with numerous patients, is that many people never grow up, never cast off immature notions and fantasies of what it means to be an adult, never achieve coherence and continuity in their sense of themselves, so what you get, ultimately, is a fake person, a simulation, a fraud.

"And these people," he continued, "can't help themselves because they don't even recognize that they are impostors. They've devoted all their energy to fooling others, and they end up also fooling themselves, victims of their own duplicity. What did Socrates tell people to do? 'Know thyself,' he said. It isn't easy to do. Also, these impostors suffer from a kind of amnesia, especially about their childhoods, when many of the foundations for their identities were established, and their adolescent periods, when they were searching desperately for acceptable identities. They forget who they were, so they are condemned to continually create new characters for themselves. It's rather sad."

"I never thought about identity that way," said Hunter. "Of course, before I met you and your colleagues, I never thought very much about identity. When I was young, like most people, I wondered what I'd end up doing with my life. But I can't say that I've even spent much time thinking about who I am or who I became. It's rather curious, if you think about it—that we spend a great deal of energy trying to figure out what other people we know or meet are like, and hardly ever think about ourselves."

"My colleagues," said Duerfklein, "still can't accept the fact that people have an unconscious and that powerful drives shape their behavior. For them, individuals don't matter very much. They're just ciphers that are of interest only when seen in groups. You could say, and this metaphor is apt since we are at sea, they are interested only in swarms of fishes and I'm interested in each individual fish. Marshall McInnis was one of the worst in that respect. He was interested in media and its effects on audiences but not on the individuals who make up an audience. And that's because it is very difficult for social scientists to deal with individuals."

"I take it you knew him. What was he like?" asked Hunter.

"Marshall and I had been good friends, but then we had a falling out. We were supposed to collaborate on a book. He stole a number of my ideas, reformulated them in his own popular style, and peddled them as his own. I felt betrayed. So if I tell you that I loathed and hated Marshall, you must understand that I have reasons for the way I feel about him. In public he was charming, and he was, I must admit, a witty and amusing fellow. But once he left the stage, he was a monster. He also was terribly immoral—actually a sad case. He was a sexual predator who felt he had to sleep with every beautiful student or other woman he met."

"How do you explain that kind of behavior?" asked Hunter. "I've met people like that and often wondered what it is that made them behave that way. You know that a famous basketball player claimed he slept with ten thousand women."

"Ha," said Duerfklein. "Ten thousand? Impossible, but it shows we're dealing with a man with grandiose notions about himself. This phenomenon is a kind of Don Juanism, sometimes called the Casanova complex, that we often see in people who have not resolved their Oedipal problems. They're searching for an ideal mother, and they have a need to dominate every woman they meet—to show their power. It's a form of obsessive-compulsive behavior, directed towards attaining as many sexual conquests as possible, perhaps to assuage anxiety one has about one's potency? Marshall had an enormous amount of energy, but it was all dissipated. You could say about him that he jumped upon a horse and galloped off in all directions at the same time. I think he felt guilty about what he had done to me, which is one of the reasons why he invited me on this cruise."

"But why did you accept?" asked Hunter. "From talking with Anastasia, Katarina, Jean-Marie, and Antonia, I take it that each of them had good reasons to despise McInnis, or even hate him. Why did any of you agree to go on this trip?"

Duerfklein smiled and looked at Hunter with an amused expression on his face.

"When dealing with people, it's best not to assume that they're always logical. Sometimes we are ambivalent about a person. On the one hand, we hate him for something he did to us, but on the other hand, we find him interesting and fascinating and are attracted to him, so we hold contradictory feelings about a person, what we psychoanalytic theorists call ambivalence. We find this played out very dramatically in young children, who at varying times both love and hate their parents. There is also the matter of conscious attitudes and unconscious ones, so ambivalence is a very tricky matter."

"I can understand that," said Hunter.

"Then, of course, individuals may be harboring grudges and looking for opportunities to get even, though they may not be conscious of that," added Duerfklein. "That often happens. Psychoanalytic theory argues that our psyches are always in conflict. Our ids, simmering cauldrons of lust and desire, are continually in conflict with our superegos, which would put us all in psychological straitjackets if they could. Mediating between the two is the ego, which is the part of our psyches devoted to helping us deal with reality and with keeping our ids and superegos in check. So wherever you look, you see unconscious forces in conflict with one another.

"If the id is too strong, people can't focus on anything. They become victims of every desire they have and flit from one thing to another. But if the id isn't strong enough, people have no energy. If the superego is too strong, people are consumed by guilt. So the ego must keep these forces in balance. When it can't, there are problems— sometimes, when the problems are very severe, people require the services of people like me. I do what I can to find ways to balance the forces that are tearing them apart. So, given the problems that we all face with conflicting elements in our psyches, it is understandable that people do things that seem strange and contradictory. We are always struggling with ourselves and our internal conflicts as much as we fight with others."

"From what you say, it seems like it's very hard to be normal," said Hunter.

"With most people, achieving a balance isn't a problem. They aren't bothered by excessive guilt or excessive desire, and they find ways to do what they have to do and are able to function tolerably well. They may not know who they are or how they arrived at their identities, but it isn't a problem for them. But with others, people whom one might describe as neurotic, these battles are all-consuming, and their identities are continually in flux. They need help from time to time. That's where Freud and Jung and Adler and Erikson and a host of others come in."

Duerfklein glanced at his watch.

"But enough of my lecturing on Freudian psychoanalytic theory. You're very patient and a good listener. It's time for dinner, and I must go back to my cabin and change. It has been a great pleasure talking with you, Solomon," he said. "We can continue this conversation at dinner, if you wish to do so."

The two men walked down the stairs from the Sun Deck and then walked by the swimming pools, where boys and girls were swimming and playing, and into the ship, where they started walking down flights of stairs.

"Good-bye," said Duerfklein, as he wandered off.

"Hmm," thought Hunter. "I wonder what he meant by that?"

From the earliest times of the first self-confidence of youth, which it is often so touching, even moving, to look back upon later, all sorts of once-loved notions lingered in his memory even today, and among them was that of "living hypothetically." This phrase still expressed the courage and the involuntary ignorance involved in a life in which every step is an act of daring without experience behind it, and the desire for large terms of reference, and the breath of revocability that is felt by a young man hesitantly entering into life. . . . A thrilling sensation of being destined to something or other is the beautiful and only certain thing in him whose gaze surveys the world for the first time. If he keeps a careful watch over his emotions he cannot say yes to anything without reservation; he seeks the possible beloved, but does not know whether she is the right one; he is capable of killing, without being sure that he must do it. His own nature's will to develop forbids him to believe in anything perfect; but everything that comes his way behaves as if it were perfect. He has a vague intuitive feeling that this order of things is not as solid as it pretends to be; nothing, no ego, no form, no principle, is safe, everything is in a process of invisible but never-ceasing transformation. . . . This is why he hesitates to become anything. (296–97)

Robert Musil, *The Man without Qualities*

Charles Brenner, *An Elementary Textbook of Psychoanalysis*

A slip of the tongue or a slip of the pen is often the consequence of a *failure* to repress completely some unconscious thought or wish. In such cases, the speaker expresses what he would have unconsciously liked to say or write, despite his attempt to keep it hidden. Sometimes the hidden meaning is openly expressed in the slip, that is to say, it is clearly intelligible to the listener or reader. On other occasions, the meaning of the lapse is not intelligible and the hidden meaning can only be discovered from the associations of the person who made the slip. (131)

chapter **fourteen**

Symphonie Wu

Hunter wasn't feeling very hungry and decided to have a light dinner at the Café del Sol on the Lido Deck. When he had selected what he wanted—some salad, roast potatoes, broccoli, and a small piece of salmon—he looked around for an empty table. To his surprise, he saw Symphonie Wu sitting by herself, at a small table by a window, looking out. She had a bowl of soup and some rice and sushi on a plate. He walked over to her table.

"Mind if I join you, Symphonie?" he said. "You look lonely, sitting here by yourself."

"Thanks for coming over," Symphonie said, glancing up at him and smiling. "My colleagues told me you're a first-class conversationalist and you're an excellent listener. That's very rare, you know."

She nibbled on some sushi.

"They're very kind," said Hunter, seating himself. "But your colleagues like to talk about their work, so I just keep the conversations going while I learn all about their ideas about identity. It is an interesting problem, isn't it? But tell me—how come you're not with your friends in the Palm Court dining hall?"

He started eating his dinner.

"I wasn't feeling very hungry this evening," she said. "I didn't sleep well last night. I hardly got any sleep. Anastasia told me about her close call. That was scary. She could have really hurt herself. She told me that shortly before her near accident, she thought she was being followed by a man with a dark mustache. That really bothered me because I could swear that man has been stalking me. And now I'm feeling a bit dizzy. I had too much for lunch. There are many temptations on this cruise that I haven't resisted as much as I should have. Those waiters are servants of the devil— no doubt about that. They bring you too much food that's too good to pass up and they urge desserts on you. I wanted to escape all that tonight."

"How are you progressing with your chapter?" asked Hunter. "Do you find it difficult to work on this ship when there are so many distractions?"

"Yes, very difficult," Symphonie replied. "I don't recall whether I told you, but I'm interested in race and identity, which is understandable since I am a person of color—according to most traditional definitions, that is. People see me as a 'yellow' woman. Most people know that one out of every four people in the world is Chinese, which leads them to think of Chinese people, generally speaking, as faceless masses of humanity, people without distinctive personalities and identities—one replaceable by another, none very much different from another. Except of course for a few politicians and a couple of movie stars."

"I take it that you're talking about stereotypes people in the West have," said Hunter.

"Yes, that's the precise term," Symphonie said. "My research suggests that there's a split in the way people in the West tend to see Chinese women—we're either beautiful but dangerous bitches, what I call 'Dragon Ladies,' or their opposite, 'Sexless Drudges.' Dragon ladies or drudges! There's no room for seeing an Asian woman as an individual, as having desires and needs and a distinctive personality. There's a kind of simpleminded template that too many people in the West fit Chinese women into. It's quite ridiculous."

"I agree," said Hunter. "I would describe you as a very beautiful woman, but you don't seem to be a dragon to me."

"Thank you," said Symphonie.

"You don't seem to be dangerous either, though, of course, I don't know you that well, and appearances can be deceiving."

Symphonie laughed.

"If you only knew," she said, smiling. "One problem, Solomon, is that when it comes to race, everything is judged against the standard of whiteness, which has assumed a kind of primacy in people's eyes. I've been influenced by the work of a black woman, bell hooks, who has written a dozen books about race and society. And there are many others who have dealt with race and with 'otherness' as well, such as an English communications scholar, Stuart Hall. So there are white people and then there are all the others—people who are not white, including people who are yellow, like me. And many others who are black or brown or whatever color you can think of. Most of the movie stars and Hollywood celebrities are white, so whiteness has become the gold standard, it would seem. And those who are not white feel a certain stigma. We can see this in America, where a very large percentage of Japanese American women marry Caucasians. These women claim that Japanese American men are boring and dull and only are interested in work and saving money. This, I would argue, is a reflection of the alienation and self-hatred these Japanese American women feel—because of their skin color. So marrying out, marrying a white man, is, then, a sign of success, of moving up, as they see things, on the social ladder. And escaping from their racial heritage. What makes this more complicated is that race is, as we say, socially constructed."

"Socially constructed? What does that mean?" asked Hunter.

"It means that people's ideas about race are based on ideas they get from society. If a person has a Chinese mother and a Caucasian father, that person is not considered white by most people but a Eurasian, a person of color. Why is this person not considered white? Because whiteness is socially constructed and is typically defined as 100 percent white, though there are quite a few people who have some small percentage of nonwhite blood in them who are so light they can pass as white, and they often do. So the damage this social construction of race does is simply incredible. Women like me—yellow women—look in the mirror and see, in our dreams, a white woman looking back at us. The same applies to black women and other women of color.

"In China, of course, everyone has yellow skin, so although we have a subliminal and unconscious jealousy of white women as the paragons of beauty, at least we don't suffer from bigotry and racial hatred. But in countries like the United States and in many countries in western Europe, Chinese children are often insulted and have a difficult time, and so they grow to hate their yellow skin. And that, more or less, is what I write about."

"When you married your late husband, Marshall McInnis, was that because you were afflicted with the same notion?" asked Hunter. "Were you trying to escape your Chinese heritage through marriage to Marshall? Was it an escape, as you might put it, from your yellowness?"

"I must confess that I hadn't thought about our relationship that way when I married him," she replied. "Marshall was a famous professor, and I was flattered that he was interested in me, and I thought I'd have a wonderful life in the United States as the wife of a famous professor. And then came the great disillusionment. In public he was a charmer and everyone's favorite, but in private, he was an egomaniacal, sex-obsessed beast. He was a very disturbed man. He justified his immoral behavior with nonsense about open marriages and that kind of thing. What a fool I was. But I was younger and not very wise. I was hypnotized by a fantasy of myself walking down the aisle in a beautiful wedding dress and being the center of attention."

"A white wedding dress, I take it," said Hunter.

"Of course," said Symphonie.

"How did you choose the name *Symphonie*?" asked Hunter. "Are you from a musical family? Do you play any musical instruments?"

"Yes," she said. "I play the piano. My English name was given to me by my mother. She loved music, though she worked as a judge. She played the violin very beautifully, and she made me study the piano. My mother and father are both dead now, sad to say. He was a doctor."

"Do you have any brothers or sisters?" asked Hunter.

"I had a younger sister," replied Symphonie. "She died recently."

"What was her name?" asked Hunter.

"Symphonie. I mean Melody. I'm feeling dizzy and all mixed up," she said.

"Was she a professor like you?" asked Hunter.

"Just the opposite," said Symphonie. "Melody was very smart and did well at college, but after she graduated she fell in with the wrong people and became a drug addict and eventually a criminal to support her habit. Then, she suddenly became ill and died a while ago. She had a heart attack and died one evening, in her apartment. I imagine her drugs weakened her heart. I found her body when I went to visit her in the morning. It was a horrible experience."

Symphonie started sobbing, softly.

"I'm sorry to have stirred up some bad memories," said Hunter, trying to comfort her.

"That's all right," she said. "It's good to talk about it. It makes you feel better, I find. And I've also got my work to keep my mind off morbid thoughts, too. I've got to finish my chapter, though. I have a sense of responsibility to my colleagues. I don't want to let them down."

"Who are you rooming with?" asked Hunter.

"Anastasia, the beautiful blonde Russian woman. We're two opposites, aren't we? A Chinese woman with black hair and a Russian blonde. She's very sweet and very affectionate, I must say. I was brushing my hair earlier, and she insisted on doing it for me. She said she loves to brush hair and added that if she had her life to live over, she'd be a cosmetologist. I found that most amusing. She was married to an Italian count, but her marriage didn't work out either. Now she's married to a Russian, I believe. Marriage isn't easy."

"Half the marriages in the United States end in divorce," said Hunter. "So a failed marriage means nothing here. We believe in serial monogamy."

"You know, of course, that Marshall had his eye on Anastasia," said Symphonie. "He was sleeping with Katarina, who thought he was going to marry her, but he ditched her to chase after Anastasia. Poor thing. It's terrible to speak ill of the dead, but Marshall's heart attack saved Anastasia from him, not that she would have been as stupid as I was. His heart attack saved Katarina, too, though she doesn't realize it. Anastasia's a very intelligent woman but not very sophisticated in matters of the heart. She's all wrapped up in her semiotics and is rather un-worldly, I'd say, from talking with her."

"What about Jean-Marie Benetton? What can you tell me about him?" asked Hunter. "I had a very interesting talk with him."

"You are very curious, aren't you? I guess people can't resist gossip and that kind of thing," said Symphonie. "You find a group of people who are working together and hear things about one or two of them, and then you want to know everything else you can find out. Human curiosity is a powerful force, a very powerful force. I can see that. Well, Jean-Marie is one of those postmodernists. Nobody really understands what postmodernism is, but Jean-Marie believes that we all live in a postmodern world and that it shapes our identities more than anything else. More than signs, more than race, more than class, more than language, and more than the psyche. More than anything. French thinkers have a sense of self-assurance that is very aggravating. You can't understand what they are talking about, but they are so full of confidence about the correctness of their ideas, so certain that they are right, that you can get carried away by their nonsense."

"I had a hard time following him, I must admit. You're correct about my being very curious," said Hunter. "It comes naturally to me. We mustn't underestimate the power of human curiosity. It was only by chance that I stumbled upon you and your colleagues. I discovered that you're all very interesting individuals and that your relationships are very complicated. So, quite naturally, I felt I simply had to find out more about everyone involved in this project of yours. And, at the same time, I'm also learning a great deal about identity, as well."

"Jean-Marie is a very nice man," said Symphonie, "and very affectionate. He's probably a genius, you know. Nobody's quite sure what he's talking about in his books and articles. That's typical, as I said, of French intellectuals. But Jean-Marie and I are just having a bit of fun together on this cruise—flirting with one another and amusing ourselves. It's all quite harmless. He's married, you know. There's no percentage in getting involved with a married man. And I don't like the idea of breaking up marriages."

"I guess a bit of fun is OK," said Hunter. "Let me ask you something about Marshall, the only member of your group I haven't had the chance to chat with. He died of a heart attack. Did he have a history of heart trouble or any other serious illnesses?"

"Not that I know of," said Symphonie. "If he had serious medical problems, he never told me. He probably wanted to shield me, and himself, from any bad news on that front. If I didn't hate him so much, I'd be sad about his death, but after the way he treated me, I simply can't feel sorry for him. I hope you won't think I'm a mean-spirited, hard-hearted woman."

Symphonie's eyes were teary and she was trembling slightly.

"Are you OK?" Hunter asked.

"Yes, yes," she replied. "I'm afraid I'm beginning to get seasick. I didn't put on a patch this morning. That was a mistake."

"Can I get one for you?" asked Hunter. "They sell them in the store."

"No, I'll go back to my cabin and get one. Then, later, I think I'll go to the show with my colleagues. There's a big musical on tonight, and we decided we'll all go together. It should be fun."

"That may do you some good," said Hunter. "It will take your mind off Marshall's death, and your sister Melody's death, as well."

"Yes, you're right," she said. She got up and, with a somewhat unsteady gait, walked out of the Café del Sol.

Hunter sat thinking, playing over the various conversations he'd had in his mind. He looked out at the sea, which had turned a bit rough. The sky was still blue, and the ocean looked incredibly beautiful. He could understand, at that moment, the grip that the sea has on people—the beauty, the serenity, the quiet.

Sigmund Freud,

"Psychoanalysis"

Erik H. Erikson, *Identity:*

Youth and Crisis

It was a triumph of the interpretative art of psycho-analysis when it succeeded in demonstrating that certain common mental acts of normal people, for which no one had hitherto attempted to put forward a psychological explanation, were to be regarded in the same light as the symptoms of neurotics: that is to say they had a *meaning*, which was unknown to the subject but which could easily be discovered by analytic means. . . . A class of material was brought to light which is calculated better than any other to stimulate a belief in the existence of unconscious mental acts even in people to whom the hypothesis of something at once mental and unconscious seems strange and even absurd. (235–36)

Identity formation employs a process of simultan-eous reflection and observation, a process taking place on all levels of mental functioning, by which the individual judges himself in the light of what he perceives to be the way in which others judge him in comparison to themselves and to a typology sig-nificant to them; while he judges their way of judg-ing him in the light of how he perceives himself in comparison to them and to types that have become relevant to him. This process is, luckily, and neces-sarily, for the most part unconscious except where inner conditions and outer circumstances combine to aggravate a painful, or elated, "identity con-sciousness."

Furthermore, the process described is always changing and developing: at its best it is a process of increasing differentiation and it becomes ever more inclusive as the individual grows aware of a widening circle of others significant to him, from the material person to "mankind." (22–23)

chapter **fifteen**

Victoria

After sitting and gazing at the ocean for a while, Hunter got up and took another stroll around the deck. He wanted to think about what he'd learned that day from the Interpol report and from his conversations.

"I know that the answer to this puzzle is in my head, somewhere," he thought, "but I don't know where to find it. Something very important slipped from my mind, but I'll find it. It's just a matter of thinking everything through. This murder case is like a song. I may have forgotten the lyrics, but the melody lingers on in my mind."

There were just a few people walking on the deck—some elderly couples, a young family with twin sons of about five who were racing about, some middle-aged women, some men and women getting a bit of exercise—so he was able to walk and think about the murder without too many distractions. It had been difficult, not being able to interrogate the professors the way he would have done had the investigation been open and official. But he had, nevertheless, managed to learn a great deal. Suddenly he stopped and slapped himself on the head.

"Of course," he said to himself. "It all makes sense now."

Then he went to his room and called the captain.

"Can you invite the people at my table to dinner tomorrow night?" he asked.

"That would be very difficult," replied Captain Lombordo, "because we've already invited passengers to my table for every meal. We invite repeat customers and special guests, and it means a great deal to them. But what about a party in the afternoon? I could easily arrange something like that."

"I think that would work just as well," said Hunter. "How about three thirty in the afternoon, in some room where we won't be disturbed?"

"That will be easy to do. I'll have someone send the invitations out immediately. I'll make it a special wine tasting. That should interest most everyone."

"Good," said Hunter. "I believe I've figured out what happened to McInnis. But let's wait and see what happens. Make sure you have a number of security people, disguised as waiters, in the room, just in case something happens."

"Of course," said Captain Lombordo. "If you've solved this case, it will be an enormous relief to me. If there were another murder on the ship, and the passengers found out, it would be a disaster."

Talcott Weems returned from dinner.

"I'm stuffed," he said. "What did me in was having two desserts. I won't make that mistake again."

He rubbed his stomach.

"Want to see the show?" he asked. "It's supposed to be really great, with lots of big production numbers. It might do you a bit of good to relax for a while."

"That's a good idea," said Hunter. They left the cabin and went to the show; then, after a short stroll around the ship, they turned in.

The *Royal Duchess* docked at Victoria the next day, around noon. When Weems and Hunter got up, a fancy invitation from the captain was waiting for each of them. The invitations had been slid under the door to the cabin.

"Hey," said Weems, opening his invitation. "Get this, Solly. We've been invited to a special wine-tasting party by the captain. I bet he has some great wine, too. And great things to eat. I'm looking forward to it. This cruise is really something else!"

After lunch, Hunter and Weems got off the *Royal Duchess* and took a long walk into Victoria. The weather was beautiful, and Victoria glistened in the sunlight. It was crowded with tourists, wandering around the streets, buying souvenirs, and enjoying themselves. They walked by the Empress Hotel, where countless numbers of tourists enjoyed its very elaborate tea service every afternoon.

"It's good to get off the ship and walk around," said Hunter. "I seem to have spent all my time either walking around that top deck of the ship or talking to the professors about their theories of identity."

"And eating, too," added Weems. "I decided I really like the Palm Court dining area and am going to have all my meals there from now on. You missed a fabulous dinner. I had this crazy mango and peach soup, then a salad. I skipped the pasta. I actually had two servings of roast beef. I couldn't help myself, Hunter. It was so good. Then I had a cherry trifle, an apple pie with ice cream, and a cup of coffee. I don't know how I managed to eat it all, but I did."

"Yes, that's true, Talcott," said Hunter. "We spend a lot of time eating, don't we? I guess that's one of the reasons why people take cruises—to eat very well. It will be hard for you to get back to your old peanut butter sandwiches when we get back, won't it?"

"This is a really lovely city," said Weems. "Any idea why it's called Victoria? After some queen or something?"

"Probably," said Hunter.

"Names are interesting," said Weems. "There's a 'victor' in *Victoria*. And a 'Dutch' in *Duchess*. I wonder if there's any significance to that kind of thing? You can find funny stuff in names, sometimes.

"I wonder if those identity professors ever deal with things like that."

"That's a good question. What's in a name? Something to think about," said Hunter. "It's possible that people's names can sometimes tell you interesting things."

After wandering around Victoria for a couple of hours, Hunter and Weems made their way back to the *Royal Duchess*. They showed their cruise cards and went to their room.

"I'll dine with you and the professors in the Palm Court this evening," said Hunter. "Remember, we've got that wine-tasting party coming up in a half hour."

"Yes," said Weems. "I'm looking forward to it."

Their conversation was interrupted by a phone call.

Hunter picked up the phone. It was the captain.

"Something remarkable has happened," said the captain. "One of the professors at your table jumped overboard."

"What?" said Hunter. "Did you say she jumped, or was she pushed?"

"She jumped," said the captain. "There were a number of people on the deck who saw what happened. She ran out of a hallway onto the deck, screaming, 'He's trying to kill me,' and jumped into the water. She wasn't in the water but a minute or two when she was picked up by one of the small boats that we have circling the ship when we're in port, to prevent terrorists from trying anything. She said something about a man with a dark mustache following her. We took her to the doctor, who took a quick look at her and said she's fine. Just a bit excited about what happened."

"Who was it?" asked Hunter.

"The Chinese woman," said the captain. "Symphonie Wu."

True identity . . . depends on the support which the young individual receives from the collective sense of identity characterizing the social groups significant to him: his class, his nation, his culture. Where historical and technological developments severely encroach upon deeply rooted or strongly emerging identities (i.e. agrarian, feudal, patrician) on a large scale, youth feels endangered, individually and collectively, whereupon it becomes ready to support doctrines offering a total immersion in a synthetic identity (extreme nationalism, racism, or class consciousness) and a collective condemnation of a totally stereotyped enemy of the new identity. The fear of a loss of identity which fosters such indoctrination contributes significantly to that mixture of righteousness and criminality which, under totalitarian conditions, becomes available for organized terror and for the establishment of major industries of extermination. Since conditions undermining a sense of identity also fixate older individuals on adolescent alternatives, a great number of adults fall in line or are paralyzed in their resistance. (93)

Erik H. Erikson, *Insight and Responsibility*

Martin Grotjahn, *Beyond Laughter: Humor and the Subconscious*

The general interest in murder has often fascinated the analytic observer. We know that deep down in our hearts we are all murderers. We are vaguely aware of this and feel guilty; while reading a mystery story we may feel as if we did it ourselves. One part of us—the part which represents our carefully repressed hostile tendencies—identifies with the murderer, while other parts of our personality may identify with the detective or even with the victim who was murdered. . . . The final victory of the moral principle over crime, the punishment and atonement for crime, enjoyed vicariously and guilt-free, makes the reading of a mystery story a permissible enjoyment against which our conscience cannot protest. (153–54)

chapter **sixteen**

PETRUS 1974 POMEROL

The Captain's Party

At 3:30 that afternoon, Hunter and Weems wandered over to the room where the party was being held. In the center of the room there was a long table with plates and four wine glasses, of different shapes, behind each plate.

Everyone from the table was seated, chatting away.

"Good to see you, Solomon," said Anastasia. "And you too, Mr. Weems. Come sit by me. There are two empty chairs for you."

Hunter and Weems sat down.

"We thought this would be a much bigger party," said Jean-Marie Benetton. "But it's only our table. So I can't help but think that it's because you're at our table. I believe you must be a very important person if the captain is throwing a party for you."

"Not really," said Hunter.

"He's right about that," said Weems. "He's not a big shot, by any means."

"I don't believe you, Talcott," said Antonia.

"How are you, Symphonie?" asked Hunter. "I heard about what happened just a while ago."

"I'm . . . I'm fine," said Symphonie. She was seated next to Jean-Marie. "I think my imagination ran away with me. But I thought this

131

man, with a dark mustache, was following me and wanted to kill me. I can see now that I was hysterical and overreacted . . . but at the time I really was terrified."

"I'm glad to hear that you're OK," said Hunter.

At that moment the captain interrupted their conversation.

"If I might have your attention for a moment," said the captain. "Our maître d' is here to serve as the wine master. He will describe the wines we have for you . . . and a very fine selection of wines he has."

"Thank you, Captain," said the maître d'. "My name is Alessandro Scelba, and I've been with the Princess line for twenty years. Captain Lombordo told me to prepare a wine tasting with our very best Bordeaux wines, and I have done so. We will also be serving caviar and other delicacies to you. I have a number of my best waiters here to take care of your every need."

Everyone at the table applauded. The waiters brought some caviar on toast and other little sandwiches and placed them on everyone's plates.

"We start with a Lafite Rothschild Pauillac 1999."

The waiters poured the wine in everyone's wine glass.

"Please smell the wine first. Notice the lovely bouquet. Then gently move your glasses in a circular motion and let the wine swish around a bit to let the aroma build. Now take a taste."

He drank a bit of the wine and smiled.

"Delicious, is it not? Tasting slightly of pears and apples, with a delicate plum and cherry aftertaste. Now we will move on to the next wine. This is a Mouton Rothschild Pauillac 1996. A big step up the ladder. It's very subtle and complex. Notice how rich and fleshy it tastes and how beautifully integrated it is, with a ripe cherry, tobacco, and plum aftertaste. And perhaps a subtle taste of pepper?"

The waiters poured the Mouton Rothschild 1996 in the second wineglass.

"Please swish your glasses again. Notice the aroma of this wine. Its nose is both subtle and delicate. Now, take a taste. It is warm on entry, smelling of black currants, cherry, and vanilla. Do you detect, perhaps, a hint of ripe plum and blueberry? I think you can see that there is a difference between this and the Lafite 1999. Both wines are superb, of course. With fine wines like these, it is often a purely subjective matter of which you prefer. This wine, in case you are interested, sells for $275 a bottle in wine stores."

"Unbelievable," whispered Weems to Hunter. "That much money for one bottle of wine. I don't think it's worth it."

"But you're not a wine snob," said Hunter in a hushed voice. "You don't live for wine the way wine snobs do."

"Now we move up several notches to a Petrus 1994 Pauillac," said Scelba. "This wine, I should inform you, is one of my favorites."

The waiters poured the Petrus 1994 into the third glass.

"Notice the color. Notice the brilliant hue and the aroma."

He sipped a bit of the wine in his glass. There was a look of utter bliss on his face.

"This wine," he continued, "is simply heavenly. It's liquid sunshine, with wonderful balance and a velvety texture. And the complex taste, rich and deeply fruited with subtle tones of oak and strawberry. Please taste your Petrus 1994."

Everyone tasted the Petrus 1994.

"Unbelievable," said Jean-Marie. "I'm from France and I know wine. This is, most certainly, the finest wine I've ever had. Formidable!"

"Yes, it is really delicious," said Symphonie. "I never realized that wine could be so delicious."

"I'm glad you like it," said Scelba. "It is, indeed, a marvelous wine. Few people have the good fortune to taste a wine such as this. But it is only a preparation for the pièce de résistance, a truly magnificent wine. Captain Lombordo, our host, has spared no expense for this wine tasting."

Everyone at the table applauded.

"Thank you, thank you," said the captain. "It is my pleasure. I am happy to offer this wine tasting to you."

"Now," said the maître d', "I offer you one of the great Bordeaux wines of the last twenty years—nothing less than a Petrus 1998 Pomerol. For those of you who are interested in such things, this wine sells for around $1,800 a bottle."

The waiters poured the Petrus 1998.

"Please swish it around your glasses for a few seconds to let the aroma build. Now, take a taste."

"Wow," said Katarina.

"Yes, 'wow' is the word," said the maître d'. "Very few people are privileged to taste such a wine. And there are no words to adequately describe it. I marvel at its delicacy, its power, its superb bouquet, its structure, its complexity, its intense and rich taste, its marvelous velvety aftertaste of plums, melons, blueberries, and black pepper. It is wildly sexy, remarkably seductive. The balance, the finish . . . marks of a truly dangerous wine. I am at a loss for words."

"Wunderbar," said Sigfried Duerfklein. "A remarkable wine. The nectar of the gods, one might say."

"Yes, yes," said the maître d', smiling. "A good way to put it. I'm delighted that you liked these wines. On the *Royal Duchess* we try to make our passengers happy. And I believe this wine tasting has done that. And now I must return to my labors, but Captain Lombordo would like to say a few words."

Everyone at the table applauded as the maître d' left the room.

"I'm very happy that you liked the wines my maître d' chose for you," said the captain. "I told him I wanted this to be a superb experience for you, and I believe it has been. Not all passengers on the *Royal Duchess* have a wine tasting such as this one, I must admit. But this wine tasting is a special occasion, and I have held it because, as some of you might have guessed, Solomon Hunter and Talcott Weems are at your table."

At this, the others at the table applauded.

"I knew you were someone important," said Katarina. "We don't know what you do, but you had a presence that we could all sense. Are you the president of this line by chance?"

"No, not at all," said Hunter. "But you're all correct. It was I who arranged to have this wine-tasting party, and I'm delighted that you all came and have been enjoying yourselves. Since you're all interested in identity, let me identify myself. You all know my name, but you don't know what I do. Now let me tell you. I'm a detective. An inspector with the San Francisco Police."

"A flic?" said Jean-Marie, in surprise.

"You don't look like a policeman," said Symphonie. "You don't dress like one, either."

"But why are you on this cruise?" asked Sigfried Duerfklein.

"Yes, what are you doing on this cruise? And why have you been dining with us?" added Antonia Fathom.

"Let me explain," replied Hunter. "We received a call from Captain Lombordo early in the afternoon of June 8, the day the *Royal Duchess* was set to sail for Alaska. He called because Marshall McInnis was found, early that afternoon, with a knife sticking in his back. He'd been murdered!"

"Murdered?" cried Anastasia. "It doesn't seem possible."

"Who could have done such a terrible thing?" said Katarina. "Was it someone on the crew?"

"What a tragedy," said Jean-Marie.

"I asked the captain," Hunter continued, "to send a message to each of you at the table saying McInnis had died of a heart attack. We did that to gain time and to make sure that rumors about someone being murdered didn't spread to the passengers and the crew. People don't like to cruise for ten days knowing there's a murderer on board their ship. Captain Lombordo asked me and Weems to take the cruise and see whether we could solve the crime. I checked with headquarters, and they OK'd it. Then the captain arranged for us to be seated at your table for the evening meal. That enabled us to get to know you. I made it a point to speak with each of you—in part because I became interested in the subject of identity that you are all working on. As a detective, I'm also extremely interested in identity, as you can well imagine. But my primary purpose was to see if I could figure out which of you might have killed McInnis."

"You mean it wasn't a crew member? One of us? Absurd," said Jean-Marie. "We're scholars. We don't go around killing people."

"As a rule, you're right. Professors don't generally murder people. But there are exceptions," said Hunter. "The problem I faced was looking for a motivation. Many of you had a reason for hating McInnis. And others might have had a reason I didn't find out about. For example, Symphonie had been married to him, and he had treated her terribly. Sigfried told me that McInnis stole his ideas. Katarina was involved with him, but he ditched her to chase after Anastasia. I could go on and on. And yet I didn't see any of these motivations as strong enough to lead someone to kill McInnis. There was nothing that important to lead to a murder that I could put my finger on."

"So why do you think one of us killed Marshall?" asked Anastasia.

"It had to do with identity, curiously enough," said Hunter. "I sent to Interpol for information about you, to see if I could find anything in your backgrounds that might be interesting. Nothing of any importance on any of you, except that I found that Symphonie had a twin sister. That interested me, of course. When I had a conversation with her, over dinner in the Café del Sol last night, the subject of her family came up, and she told me she had a younger sister who had died."

"That's true," said Symphonie.

"Yes, you were telling me the truth, in a sense. But your sister was actually a twin sister, born an hour before you were born. This sister, you said, had graduated from college and then fallen in with the wrong crowd, become a drug addict, and ended up a criminal. So we have twin sisters—one is a scholar and very intellectual, and the other is a criminal with a long record."

"Poor thing," said Jean-Marie. "It must have been very difficult for you, Symphonie."

Symphonie nodded. She had a very sad, perhaps even frightened, look on her face.

"What happened, I concluded, is that it was the scholarly sister, Symphonie, who died, and this woman here—who claims to be Symphonie—is really her twin sister, Melody. She's been impersonating Symphonie since she died."

"No, no, you're wrong," said Symphonie.

"When I was chatting with you, I asked you your sister's name. You said 'Symphonie,' then switched it to 'Melody.' That confirmed my hypothesis, as you professors might put it."

"I was ill," Symphonie said. "I was dizzy and confused."

"What probably happened is that McInnis invited you to his stateroom to discuss your chapter, discovered, somehow, that you weren't Symphonie, and threatened to expose you, so you killed him. You had escaped from your old identity, that of a criminal, and were enjoying your new life as a professor. You couldn't bear to face being exposed and, in an act of desperation, stuck a knife in McInnis's back. He'd ordered a steak dinner earlier, and it was easy for you to grab the knife and kill McInnis. Who knows? It might not have been the first time you killed someone!"

"I'd kill you, if I could," she snarled. "You're right. Symphonie died suddenly—I didn't do it. She had a weak heart—so I grabbed the chance to trade identities. She had finished writing a number of articles and a book manuscript, so I was able to take advantage of that, and I boned up on this identity business. It was pretty easy to fool everyone. You learn a bit of jargon, read a few articles and a couple of books, and, to make things easier, Symphonie was on sabbatical for a year after she died." She suddenly burst out crying.

"I lost my head. That bastard McInnis figured out, right away, that I wasn't Symphonie. He threatened to expose me unless I had sex with him. I said no, but then he grabbed me and threw me on his bed and forced himself on me. So, in a fit of madness, I killed him. He was lying in bed, resting. Maybe even dozing. So I stuck a knife in his back. I cleaned off all my fingerprints and slipped out of the cabin. I thought that Anastasia was walking in the hallway and noticed me leaving his cabin. I was afraid that Anastasia might eventually figure out what happened and tell someone what she saw, so I tried to silence her, tripping a lady who went crashing into Anastasia when she was at the top of a flight of stairs. Then, when I heard about the guy with the dark mustache, I thought I'd fake being attacked, to throw suspicion off myself."

"I'm sorry, but we're going to have to arrest you for the murder of Marshall McInnis," said Hunter. "The captain will place you in custody, and then, when we return to San Francisco, you'll be tried for McInnis's murder."

Melody Wu started sobbing and shaking as she was led away.

Everyone at the table sat there, stunned by the developments.

"So, we were all wrong about you," said Anastasia. "I can tell you now that I thought you were an executive, and Katarina thought you might be a surgeon. Jean-Marie thought you were a lawyer, and Sigfried said he thought you were in advertising or something like that. Poor Marshall. Though you could say he had it coming to him. I could well believe that he raped Symphonie. Or Melody. Or whoever she is."

"The autopsy indicated that McInnis had had sex shortly before he died. I think there's a good chance that Melody will be found innocent because she was raped," said Hunter. "Or given a light sentence. In situations such as this, juries tend to be most forgiving."

"I hope so," said Jean-Marie. "And maybe she'll be able to do something with her life. She is, after all, an intelligent woman—and a daring one, too."

"That's very possible," said Sigfried Duerfklein. "One thing we know is that, given the right circumstances, people can change, and experiences such as the one that this poor woman had on this cruise can

lead to major alterations in one's personality and life. I wouldn't be surprised if this woman does something with her life after this ordeal is
over. She no longer needs to be an impostor, so all things are possible."

"I propose a toast," said Antonia. She raised her glass.

"To hope and to the future. And to identity!"

biblio**graphy**

Allport, Gordon W. *Becoming: Basic Considerations for a Psychology of Personality*. New Haven, CT: Yale University Press, 1955.

Barthes, Roland. *A Lover's Discourse: Fragments*. Trans. Richard Howard. New York: Hill and Wang, 1978.

———. *Mythologies*. Trans. Annette Lavers. New York: Hill and Wang, 1972.

Benetton, Jean-Marie. *Constructing the Postmodern Self: Gender, Sex, Body, and the Creation of Identities*. Trans. Arthur Asa Berger. Ann Arbor: University of Michigan Press, 2000.

Benoist, Jean-Marie. *Marx est mort*. Paris: Gallimard, 1970.

Berger, Arthur Asa. *Bloom's Morning: Coffee, Comforters, and the Secret Meaning of Everyday Life*. Boulder, CO: Westview, 1997.

———. *Durkheim Is Dead: Sherlock Holmes Is Introduced to Sociological Theory*. Walnut Creek, CA: AltaMira Press, 2003.

Bettelheim, Bruno. *The Uses of Enchantment: The Meaning and Importance of Fairy Tales*. New York: Knopf, 1976.

Brenner, Charles. *An Elementary Textbook of Psychoanalysis*. Garden City, NY: Anchor, 1974.

Butler, Judith. *Bodies That Matter: On the Discursive Limits of Sex*. New York: Routledge, 1993.

————. *Gender Trouble: Feminism and the Subversion of Identity*. Tenth anniversary edition. New York: Routledge, 1999.

Dennis, Nigel. *Cards of Identity*. New York: Vanguard, 1955.

Dickson, Bob, and Andy Vladimir. *Selling the Sea: An Inside Look at the Cruise Industry*. New York: Wiley, 1997.

Duerfklein, Sigfried. *The Secret Self: The Psychology of the Impostor*. Cambridge, MA: Harvard University Press, 2004.

————. *Studies in the Creation of an Identity: An Introduction*. 3 volumes. New York: Routledge, 1998.

Durham, Meenakshi Gigi, and Douglas M. Kellner, eds. *Media and Cultural Studies: KeyWorks*. Malden, MA: Blackwell, 2001.

Erikson, Erik H. *Identity: Youth and Crisis*. New York: Norton, 1968.

————. *Insight and Responsibility*. New York: Norton, 1964.

Fathom, Antonia. *The Rhetoric of Identity*. Oxford: Blackwell, 2003.

Fausto-Sterling, Anne. *Sexing the Body: Gender Politics and the Construction of Sexuality*. New York: Basic Books, 2000.

Ferguson, Marjorie, and Peter Golding. "Cultural Studies and Changing Times: An Introduction." In *Cultural Studies in Question*, ed. Marjorie Ferguson and Peter Golding. London: Sage, 1997.

Foucault, Michel. *The History of Sexuality: An Introduction*. New York: Vintage, 1980.

Freud, Sigmund. *Group Psychology and the Analysis of the Ego*. In *A General Selection from the Works of Sigmund Freud*, ed. John Rickman. Garden City, NY: Anchor, 1957.

————. "Psychoanalysis." In *Character and Culture*, ed. Philip Rieff. New York: Collier, 1963.

Fromm, Erich. *Beyond the Chains of Illusion: My Encounter with Marx and Freud*. New York: Simon & Schuster, 1962.

Goffman, Erving. *Relations in Public: Microstudies of the Public Order*. New York: Harper, 1971.

————. *Stigma: Notes on the Management of Spoiled Identity*. Englewood Cliffs, NJ: Prentice-Hall, 1963.

Gorer, Geoffrey, and John Rickman. *The People of Great Russia: A Psychological Study*. New York: Norton, 1962.

Grotjahn, Martin. *Beyond Laughter: Humor and the Subconscious*. New York: McGraw-Hill, 1966.

Jagose, Annamarie. *Queer Theory: An Introduction*. New York: New York University Press, 1997.

Kellner, Douglas M., and Meenakshi Gigi Durham. "Adventures in Media and Cultural Studies: Introducing KeyWorks." In *Media and Cultural Studies: KeyWorks*, ed. Meenakshi Gigi Durham and Douglas M. Kellner. Malden, MA: Blackwell, 2001.

Klapp, Orrin E. *The Collective Search for Identity*. New York: Holt, Rinehart and Winston, 1969.

Kosofsky, Eve. *Epistemology of the Closet*. Berkeley: University of California Press, 1992.

Le Bon, Gustave. *The Crowd*. 1888. New York: Viking, 1960.

Lotman, Anastasia. *Markers: The Semiotics of Identity*. Moscow: Pelmenyi Press, 2003.

MacCannell, Dean. *The Tourist: A New Theory of the Leisure Class*. New York: Schocken, 1976.

Mittags, Katarina. *MedienMarx*. Hamburg, Germany: Europaische Verlagsanstalt, 2000.

Musil, Robert. *The Man without Qualities*. New York: Capricorn, 1965.

Parsons, Talbot, and Talula Smedley Parsons. *The Sociological Perspective*. 8th ed. Keokuk, IA: Hogstate Press, 2004.

Pynchon, Thomas. *The Crying of Lot 49*. New York: Bantam, 1966.

Rogers, Raymond. *Coming into Existence: The Struggle to Become an Individual*. New York: Delta, 1967.

Ruitenbeek, Hendrik M. *The Individual and the Crowd: A Study of Identity in America*. New York: Mentor, 1965.

Simmel, Georg. *Simmel on Culture*. Ed. David Frisby and Mike Featherstone. London: Sage, 1997.

Slater, Shirley, and Harry Basch. *Fielding's Alaska Cruises*. Redondo Beach, CA: Fielding Worldwide, 1997.

Steeves, Leslie H., and Marilyn Crafton Smith. "Class and Gender in Prime-Time Television Entertainment: Observations from a Socialist Feminist Perspective." *Journal of Communication Inquiry* 11, no. 1 (Winter 1987): 43–63.

Stein, Maurice, Arthur J. Vidich, and David Manning White, eds. *Identity and Anxiety: Survival of the Person in Mass Society*. New York: Free Press, 1960.

Wildavsky, Aaron. "Conditions for a Pluralist Democracy, or Cultural Pluralism Means More Than One Political Culture in a Country." Mimeographed paper, 1982.

Winick, Charles. *Desexualization in American Life*. New Brunswick, NJ: Transaction, 1995.

Wu, Symphonie. *Yellow Skin, White Soul*. Boston: Houghton Mifflin, 2002.

about the **author**

Arthur Asa Berger is professor emeritus of broadcast and electronic communication arts at San Francisco State University, where he taught between 1965 and 2003. He graduated in 1954 from the University of Massachusetts, where he majored in literature and philosophy. He received an M.A. degree in journalism and creative writing from the University of Iowa in 1956. He was drafted shortly after graduating from Iowa and served in the U.S. Army in the Military District of Washington in Washington, DC, where he was a feature writer and speechwriter in the district's Public Information Office. He also covered high school sports for the *Washington Post* on weekend evenings.

Berger spent a year touring Europe after he got out of the army and then went to the University of Minnesota, where he received a Ph.D. in American studies in 1965. He wrote his dissertation on the comic strip *Li'l Abner*. In 1963–1964, he had a Fulbright to Italy and taught at the University of Milan. He spent a year as visiting professor at the Annenberg School for Communication at the University of Southern California, in Los Angeles, in 1984.

He is the author of numerous articles and book reviews and more than fifty books on the mass media, popular culture, humor, and everyday life. Among his books are *Media and Society*, *Media and Communication*

Research Methods, *The Art of Comedy Writing*, and *Video Games: A Popular Culture Phenomenon*. He has also written a number of comic academic mysteries. His books have been translated into seven languages, and he has lectured in more than a dozen countries in the course of his career.

Berger is married, has two children and three grandchildren, and lives in Mill Valley, California. He enjoys going to the theater, foreign travel, and dining in ethnic restaurants. He can be reached by e-mail at either arthurasaberger@gmail.com or arthurasaberger@yahoo.com.